MY VISION

A Journey through Biblical Truth

JOSEPH N. PADILLA

To order additional copies of this book, contact:
Proisle Publishing Services LLC
1177 6th Ave 5th Floor
New York, NY 10036, USA
Phone: (+1 347-922-3779)
info@proislepublishing.com

PROISLE PUBLISHING

My Vision–A Journey through Biblical Truth.

The vision given to me by God, I will try to inter-pret and make it simple to understand. It is the story of abomination that happened onto the day Noah entered the ark. This concerns me to what is happening today and the future of man to come. Is it a repeat of what is written in **Mathew 24:37:" But as the days of Noah were, so shall the coming of the Son of man be."**

What about those days of Noah before the flood? It is written that they were drinking, taking of sub- stances, marrying, and giving onto lust man leaving the natural use of woman burned in their lust toward one another, man with man with acts against nature. Filled with unrighteousness, fornication, wickedness, murder, and full of envy; haters of God openly on to the day Noah entered the ark. So, shall it be onto the coming of the Lord.

No! No man knoweth the time or the day only God the Father.

Table of Contents

Book 1

Part 1   A Place Called Heaven...3

Part 2   When Will the Fall of Men come?.......................19

Part 3   Parables and Definitions of the Bible 25

Part 4   Be Still and Know That I Am God.....................33

Part 5   The Battle of Man and Spirit Begins..................37

Part 6   Turning to Please Men...41

Part 7   Let's move on, God's Word, the Bible. 43

Part 8   Who is Killing the King James Bible? 49

Part 9   Where Do We Go from Here? 51

Part 10 Why Did Jesus Come to Earth? 53

Part 11 Where Are We?..55

Book 2

Part 12 Noah Before the Flood 65

Part 13 A Man Called Noah 69

Part 14 A Time to Start–A Time to Rip. 79

Part 15 A Welcome to the New World 89

Part 16 "You Must Move On." 95

Part 17 A New Life Beyond the Lake...............................99

About the Author 103

My Name is Joseph N. Padilla....................................103

Part 1
My Vision of the
The King James Bible

Part 2
Genesis: Before the Flood
By Joseph N. Padilla

Book 1

# Part 1

A Place Called Heaven

Once in empty space that was hidden by darkness without form and void, the Spirit of the Holy Ghost separated light throughout that which He, God, created. God called the ferment Heaven (what we know as the universe). The Creator saw that it was good. In Heaven was the deity, what we know as the Godhead: The Father, the Son, and the Holy Ghost. **(Romans 1:20)**

God saw that it was good. But, it was not com- pleted within! He created angels with such beauty; these spirits were His angelic children.

Amongst the deep darkness, in the center of the uni- verse, God saw a beauty that men cannot explain. The Spirit of God moved upon the face of the waters (space). The stages of creation called days were not periods of twenty-four hours as we know them, for there was no sun to regulate time as we know it, and with the Lord, a day is as a thousand years, and one thousand years as a day.

The first words of the Lord in the process of creation were, "Let there be light" and there was light. He saw the beauty of the heavenly lights in the vest space He called heaven.

Amongst the heavenly bodies was a blue form in the center of all. The planet we call the earth. it stood without form, so translucent and beautiful. God called it Earth. God saw everything was good. With my cre- ative mind, let's pretend the stars were without move- ment, so the star we call the sun stood still and the back of the planet we call Earth was in cold darkness, and God said, ***I will make movement upon the dark- ness.*** So, done: the heavenly bodies were in motion.

God called the light "day" and the dark side He called "night" **(Genesis 1:20)**.   The morning and the evening of the fourth day, God saw the water of the sea upon the surface of the earth and how beautiful the aqua- marine colors were; so, He created aquatic creatures so beautiful to fulfill their inhabitance therein.

But, the firmament upon the midst of the water was without formation. God gathered all the ferment together and called it Earth. This is the only astronom- ical object known to harbor lifeform. It was so done. God formed a garden on the east side of the planet Earth and He named the garden and called it Eden. God called the dry land "Earth" and the waters "the sea" and filled its surface with many creatures and fowl that He loved so dearly to inhabit therein.

In this paradise God called Eden, the Lord saw that it was good, but, the beasts that roamed freely were not able to tend the garden he called Eden. God needed a special caregiver to tend and enjoy the glory that He had made.

Knowing that Eden was without a caregiver, God said, ***"I will make a human form that I will call man."*** So out of the dust of the ground, God formed man after their image (the Father, the Son, and the Holy Spirit). The first man became his family here on Earth. God gave the man a name. He called him "Adam" (meaning "earth"; in Hebrew *Ad-amah*). God gave Adam domain over all plants and all the animals. Adam named them all one by one. Before all this took place, let's go to the beginning. In heaven was an archangel named Lucifer. He was the most perfect and beautiful angel in heaven; he had much power over all the other angels; one can say his power was rigorous, and this power went to his head, thinking he was a god with equal power of God Jehovah.

War broke out in heaven. Michel the archangel and his army of angels fought with the one called Lucifer now called "Devil" and "Satan." With this sin, he was cast out from a celestial heaven to unknown destina- tion beyond our comprehension. **Revelation 12:9** says he was casted to the earth before man's creation took place; his angels were cast down with him and the gates of heaven were closed behind him and his angels.

Here on Earth, the first man called Adam was placed in God's garden called Eden as the caretaker. The Lord God said*, "It is not good that man should be alone; I will make a help meet (mete) for him"* **(Genesis**

2:18). The Lord God caused a deep sleep to fall upon Adam, and He took one of his ribs and from the rib the Lord God had taken from man, made He a woman, and brought her unto the man **(Genesis 2:21-22).** Adam named her Eve (meaning "mother of life").

They both roamed freely in the garden east of Eden. The Holy Spirit covered their naked bodies with inno- cence and they were not ashamed **(Genesis 2:25).** They roamed freely with one exception that God had com- manded, that the tree that stood in the garden, known as the tree of life, and the tree of knowledge of good and evil, He, saying, *"Of every tree of the garden you may eat freely, but, of the tree of knowledge you shall not eat; for the day you eat of it you shall surely die"* **(Genesis 2:16-17).** Unknown to Adam and Eve what it meant when God said, **"You will surely die,"** Adam knew it had to do with disobeying God's word.

Satan, snooping nearby, heard the commandment God give to Adam and Eve. Satan, being of a jealous spirit, was standing by the way knew he had to pry and interfere getting involved and doing something con- niving to Adam and Eve.

One afternoon in the beauty of the day, Adam and Eve were enjoying and eating the fruits of the garden, when Lucifer, very shrewd, showing sharp powers of as that of a serpent, full of jealousy and anger, ready to strike, approached Adam and Eve claiming to be most knowledgeable, told Eve as she stood nearby **"that she will not surely die"** and that her eyes would open with much knowledge and she would be as knowledgeable as God, knowing all, good and evil.

Adam and Eve knew Lucifer was one of God's beloved angels with much knowledge, not knowing what transformation of disobedience that Lucifer had gone through with God. Eve so convinced, she also convinced Adam and heeded to Lucifer's command and disobeyed God's commandment; they ate of the for- bidden fruit. At that very moment, the bright light of the Holy Spirit that covered their naked bodies with innocence was removed and shame came upon Adam and Eve, both knowing that their eyes had opened to an unfamiliar event that they had never experienced.

A different feeling came upon them when touching and looking at their bodies. They stood looking at each other with guilt and shame, and they commenced, cov- ering their bodies with leaves in fear that God would see their nakedness. From that day on, the serpent released its venom ready to strike with sin and death.

Lucifer, now called Satan or Devil, has had the door of heaven closed from him forever. Death and sorrow overtook man, unable to judge right from wrong, and unable to understand the grief they had caused God. As time passed on, men turned to the world of sin and greed, and as they moved forward, men became distant from God, and both men and beast became ravenous with much disobedience (sin).

The animals they loved so dearly, like the lion and the bears and other forms of beasts (possibly the dino- saurs) unknown to us had become unfriendly and dan- gerous and started to devour one another, becoming flesh eaters, and the humans were unable to come near them. Even the gentle animals like the deer and the birds would steer away from them, the birds would fly away, the serpent (snake) became venomous, striking small creatures and became a flesh (meat) eater.

The world had changed, and the loss of the faithful descendants had distanced themselves away as they separated from each other on to the time of Noah. There, after the Lord God inspired men to speak and record His word from one generation to another. God's law, the commandments in pre-Noah time had to have been like The Ten Commandments today.

All this has been passed down by word of mouth, with art, etchings, and some of the works that men had gathered; much of this was lost in time.

It is unknown if the testaments of God were spoken publicly back then. Could this be the reason why none have been found? As far as we know, the first etchings ever found were written on clay slates. All this is pre- historic with no other evidences other than fossils of creatures that roamed the earth possibly before the flood, and with other evidence that has been found before Noah's time. **For God wiped all traces of a world gone badly.**

Men had one language. Sometime after the flood, God confused the language at Babylon a major city of ancient Mesopotamia. Babylonian ruins lie today in a modern-day Iraq. God has given me a vision and I feel that my writings in this manuscript are inspired by the inspiration of The Holy Spirit.

I will give you my interpretation and my under- standing of the parables and how I interpret them. I will start with **Genesis 3:1.** What is meant by "the serpent in the garden"? No, not a snake. The serpent is but an embodied symbol of Satan, a wild clever and malicious angel. There was no way in those days to describe something so frightful as the serpent had become on that day Adam and Eve disobeyed the Lord and did eat the forbidden fruit, for the serpent strikes its prey without warning, as Satan does also. The ser- pent was more cunning than any beast of the field the Lord had made. Now go to **Revelation 12:9. "So the great dragon was cast out, that serpent of old, called the devil and Satan, who deceives the whole world."** Next read **Revelation 20:2: "He had laid hold of the dragon, that serpent of old, who is the Devil; once a beloved angel of God."**

Satan is wily, shrewd, and full of clever tricks, crafty, treacherous, and a malicious spirit called ser- pent, dragon, or devil, which creeps so quietly like a snake before he strikes. And the Lord said unto the serpent (Satan), ***"Because thou hast done this, thou art cursed above all cattle, and above every beast of the field; upon thy belly, shall thou go, and dust shall thou eat all the days of your life"*** **(Genesis 3:14).** I will try to interpret this parable in the simple way I see it.

The serpent represents a low-down spirit that ven- tures along the ground we walk on, where blood and death of disciples and of man had spilled into the dust of the wind (a paraphrase of what I believe God said that day to Satan).

"Covered with the dust of the wind, (sins of the world) ***and with the discomfort and disgrace that you have placed upon men, there you shell dwell in the heat in the center of the earth, a place I call the lake of fire."*** Symbolic: this is the only place known to men that can be described as "hot as hell," referred to a place of eternal punishment, unknown to men (here on Earth).

Satan, alias Lucifer, was exiled from heaven and the Garden of Eden; now the devil is known as the prince of the air with no place to hide from God. Satan lures in places where one would least expect it, even in the most sacred places.

With kindness, the Lord gave men freewill and a new beginning. Men have a choice between good and evil, for Satan knows that men have lost their rea- soning, for the mind of men is no longer innocent, but corrupt. Men became intellectual and that opened the door to men's greed. Filled with power and greed, men became so powerful that all nations have a leader, and this causes war after war. The power of men became so powerful that men became slaves to those with power. Seeking freedom from slavery, men turned to God for guidance; this came about in the time of Moses. Slavery was men's most fearful thought.

God saw the behavior of man and decided to send His only begotten Son, Jesus, and He too was deceived, and crucified by His own people whom He loved so dearly, that He took all our sins to the cross, so we may be born again in the spirit of God into eternal life; all you must do is believe in Him and do His will.

It is easy to say, "I'm saved," but have you done His will? Do you love those who persecute you? And those who need your help to the best of your ability, looking down at those who live on the streets? Place yourself down and out without a job and having to walk the streets begging for help and can't get a job because they don't have a permanent place of residence. Many don't seem to care if you are a veteran who has come home from war or an unfortunate person with no skills walking the streets. Hypocrites don't curse the down and out; you must pray for them, be grateful, and count your blessings; you have a roof over your head, food on the table, and a coat on your back.

We are so confused in this world. We have been sur- rounded with evil from the beginning of time. We listen to man and not to God. Though corrupted, man can reason with himself and realize that with faith, man can restore his rebirth in Christ Jesus. Jesus said, ***"I am the***

resurrection and the life; he who believes in me, though he were dead, (dead in the word.*) **yet he shall live"** (John 11:25).

I am known as Joseph by those who know me; as for my background, I am a common person. I am not a highly-educated person, nor a student of the ministry, but I am a brother in the Word of God; my eyes have been open with something wonderful. As for my knowl- edge of the Bible, it is mostly self-taught, with the help of my Lord God Jehovah, my parents, and my grand- mother who is British and was an English teacher in parochial school. She taught me English in a Victorian way, as to where I could distinguish the meanings of the yea's and thee.

Those are wording many people know but refuse to use them because it makes them look dumb and old fashioned by the new generation of today's linguist.

Some say the KJV (King James Bible) language is not advanced enough, and that common words mean something else; this may be why so many folks don't want to use the KJV, and man is trying to interpret common words to mean something totally different of what a common word that was intended to be used to express what is known back then as common English. Today words are being changed with modern words not spoken 2,000 years back.

Times have change, but the Word of God is for- ever. I try to stay away from the so-called new Bibles that have changed the wording of the KJV. The KJV is translated out of the original tongues (languages) and with the former translations diligently compared and revised.

From around 1950, there have been so many dif- ferent so-called Bibles trying to change the wording of God by saying the KJV is too hard to understand. On the contrary, this Bible is a fifth-grade level wording, and has been around for a long time without need of removal of words and verses as those so-called new Bibles. They are covering the copyrights of their new Bibles to **make money;** even if it includes the taking away and removal of God's Word.

Be careful about the satanic powers that can and will deceive you. Any good Bible teacher can easily explain the words therein without having to change the words handed down to us by the scribes of the disciples of God that have come down through the ages. Although many of the theologians of today say the KJV in not perfect, however, the KJV tells you what has been interpreted from the many sacred scrolls of time passed.

Today, we have so many Bibles that have been written and are confusing many from the true Word of God. There are over seventy-two new versions of the Bible that are becoming to be the new international interpretation of the Word, known as The World Bible that is to come; we now have The New Way Bible, The International Bible, the NEB, The New World Transition, and the New International Version, called the NIV, which is taking over most of the Bibles today. So many other so-called Bibles that are missing so many words and verses and adding new words that mean something different from God's **Word, the Bible. The NIV tells you what you want to hear! The KJV tells you what you <u>should</u> hear.**

None of the Bibles I have mentioned here—the NIV, NLT, and NKJV—none of these so-called new Bibles use the true name of God; Jehovah.

Jehovah is found **only** in **the King James Version Bible in the following books: Exodus 17:15, Judges 6:24, Psalm 83:18, Isaiah 12:2, and Isaiah 26:4.** All other Bibles replaced the word **Jehovah** with the word "Lord."

Many men are called lord; just because Lord is spelled with a capital later doesn't give you the right to omit His name of Jehovah in the Bible.

The New King James Bible is the closest to the KJV. But, it also needs interoperation, for this Bible also has many new words found in the **new world Bibles, including removal of the word "Jehovah."** Though all the verses are there and supposed to be somewhat easier to understand. But, I still recommend the King James Bible side by side for you to understand. The word **"international"** means **"the new world order"** that is to come.

Folks be aware of those so-called Bibles; if you can find it in your heart get rid or put aside your NIV, NAS, NLT, and so on. Again, I'm not saying not to read them, but all those books are missing so many important verses, and whole lines, using words that could mean different things when you look up words in the new dictionaries that are misunderstood by many common people.

After the 1960s, new words have been added with different interpretations of a common word that have a new meaning in today's world, and those less educated persons who only listen and take the words spoken by the new pastors reading from one of those new Bibles. Let's look at the book of Revelation for what is to come. The NIV has replaced the word **"testify"** with the word **"warn",** which means to advise.

These two words have different meanings. The KJV says: **"For I testify** (witness) **onto man that heareth the words of this prophecy of this book, if any man shall add unto those things, God shall add unto him the plagues that are written in this book (Revelation 22:18).** "Testify" means to bear wit- ness – truth; next, read **Revelation 22:19. "And if any man shall take away from the words of the book of this prophecy. God shall take away his part out of the book of life, and out of the Holy City, and from the thing which are written in this book."**

The NIV says, "God will take from him his share from the **tree of life** and the holy city." **Tree** is not the Book of Life. Let's look up book of life in the KJV: **"And who so ever was not found written in the book of life was cast into the lake of fire" (Revelation 20:15).**

The tree of life is not found in **Revelation 20:15.** Those books called Bibles may sound good and easy, but those books are someone telling their interopera- tion and making them sound so good by removing so many words and making the verses shorter. Again, I am not saying for you not to read them, but, it is not the whole Word of God to be teaching anyone who only listens and doesn't read. Back up and read Revelation 20:15 again.

I'm here neither to teach nor to make friends, but to show the way to the true Word of God: as I have been blessed with an understanding to share. Just read the Bible I call the KJV. Again, it has no added words or verses missing.

Those new books publishers are like wolves in sheep's clothing by using new words found in the inter- national Bibles of today. They are in it for the money, making their Bibles sound so great and easy to read, but if you look at new Bibles of today, they use words much different that could also mean something else, and misleading new upcoming Christians who are nothing but listeners and are without much education or knowledge of the teaching of the Bible.

You preachers that use those Bibles of today go back to your school; this time try using the KJV side by side and see how many things you are missing.

Don't listen to the theologians of today, who taught you what another man taught him. This is man teaching man. Your job is to teach the true Gospel, not to cut it short with new wordings of today, because you believe that the old English is old fashioned and is not accept- able when looking up files in the new words of today's way of teaching, replacing so many words that remove the true meaning of what the gospel is teaching you.

Now listen to what Jesus said: ***"Take heed that no man deceives you. For many shall come in my name, saying, I am Christ: and shall deceive man"*** **(Matthew 24:4-5). Next go to (Mark 13:21-22): "For false Christ's and false *prophets* shall rise and shall show signs and wonders to seduce if it were pos- sible, even the elect."** Those books are great stories, but not the true words of God to be called the true Holy Bible. These are just Bible stories told that have been misunderstood to what God has intended to do by sending His disciples, His apostles, and His beloved Son Jesus to teach. This is like having a half map trying to reach the Holy City, but the main part of the map is missing. Money is being made with these anti- christ books; some Christians call them satanic books.

So many Christians misinterpret the way the KJV is to be interpreted. Some eighty percent of Christian schools do not believe in the King James Bible. Go see the movie, "Got is Not Dead." This movie is a good example. The words in the KJV never change. The KJV is slowly being replaced by those antichrist books by a large percentage of fifty-three percent; it's mainly the NIV that is missing so many important words and verses spoken and written by Jesus and His apos- tles—a total over **64,575 omissions.**

Place the NIV or any other so-called new Bibles with the KJV side by side and see for yourself. In the KJV, you don't need footnotes to explain what the words or verses mean as in the new Bibles of today. Want proof, go to You-tube (google) and look up KJV vs. NIV, Pastor Dowell, or FWB Pastor Mike Haggard, one of the best is Gail Rip-linger (*New Age Bible Versions*, name of her new book), or anyone else mentioned therein.

After a friend read my blog, he told me why I don't look this up on Goggle, so I did. Warning: What I am about to tell you is true. The NIV copyright is owned and published by Zondervan publishers (a Harper Collins publisher of San Francisco that supports gay and gender movement) who also owns **the Satanic Bible copyrights and witchcraft book's** copyright. For those of you who don't believe what I am saying, look this up for yourself; go to the internet and Google and see who owns the copyrights to the NIV Bible, who also owns the satanic Bible copyright. Remember it's up to you which road you take.

A woman named Virginia Mallinckrodt is one of the editors for Harper Collins who is a lesbian with four others who helped write and interpret the NIV saying God is not a male image of man, though **Genesis 1:27** says, **"So God created man in his own image, in the image of God created he him, male and female cre- ated He them."** Yet, Mallinckrodt says that He (God) is neither a he nor a she; in their eyes God is an "**it**" (I don't know how else to describe her image of God); she has also taken the word "God" out over forty times in the NIV. Once again, look this up for yourself.

Now know this, **"You cannot drink the cup of the Lord and the cup of demons" (1 Corinthians 10:21).** Choose the right Bible. The Zondervan publishers don't care what you buy as long you buy one or the other. Zondervan also prints the King James Bible, which I bought, and it is the KJV.

But, remember they don't care what books they publish or sell; they are in it for the money; anyone can print the KJV because it has **no copyrights** as the NIV and other so-called Bibles have. You cannot copy or change any of their words in those so-called Bibles; now know this: the author of the Holy Bible is **God,** and only God Himself has the right to change or alter the Holy Bible.

God Himself gave mankind a warning. **Not to add nor to take away from His word.** The NIV has removed more than 64,575 words including the words Jehovah, Calvary, Holy Ghost, Hell, and many other vital words. Salvation comes by faith, not by men.

"Beware of prophets which come to you in sheep's clothing, but inwardly are ravening wolfs" (Matthew

7:15). And be aware of today's Bible studies with those who use and teach out of those antichrist books, called new Bibles that sound so sweet and loving but don't coincide (agree) with the word of the commandments given to us by God. Even if I tell you how I feel, it's up to you to seek the true Word of God written in the book we call the KJV.

You teachers beware of how you lead the sheep to slaughter, saying how much you love God and teaching out of one of these corruptible books called the Bible that take out and replacing so many words and lines not mention therein. Those teachings are not the teaching of the Holy Bible; I do not say not to read them but read the KJV side by side so that you will see what is missing.

"So, faith comes by hearing, and, hearing through the (true) word of God" (Romans 10:17). Not by the word of man, who are in it for money; but by the oldest scroll's known to men from the beginning that started in the Garden of Eden and continued after the flood. I, in no way, can change or alter your way of thinking; that's between you and God. Praying for salvation for all of us is my hope with my wittings. I cannot judge, for it is said, **"Thou hypocrite! First take the plank out your own eye and then you will see clearly" (Matthew 7:5). "For with what judgment you judge, you will be judged also" (Matthew 7:2).**

Know this: with God it is love (truth); with man, it is confusion and death. Don't just read the Bible, study it, one verse at a time; this way you will know what the word is saying to you.   Many folks have said the KJV is not well explained and the English language of old has changed; the only things I see that have changed are the people who want to be more intellectual than a commoner by using their superior knowledge of new wordings with one who is lack of today's modern edu- cation;

changing words to mean something so different from common words that have come down through the generations of time.

What about the person who listens to his spiri- tual concessions given to man by God? That is his right to know.

Don't insult those who praise the Lord differently than you; you may see the apple tree flourishing with red apples, but, to another person, the apples look golden yellow, but they are still apples. Remember the tree has many branches, as it is with religion. The Lord, who has given us free will, saw the vision of man mis- understanding His Word.

Why did Jesus come to the world? Religion is mis- representing Christianity; Christianity is not the law of Moses; that law has been replaced by the blood of Jesus some 2,000 years passed, who came to teach us to love one another, so why are so many religious groups calling themselves Christian by a religious denomination name? I will name some alphabetically: Adventist, Baptist, Catholic, Evangelical, Free Will Baptist, Jehovah's, Lutheran, Methodist, Pentecostal, Presbyterian Quakers, Scientologist—the list goes on; all say their way of believing is the only way to get to heaven.

I have visited many churches of all denominations who tell me about how the other churches are so wrong, calming salvation and judging others; oh, you hypo- crites, open your Bibles and look this up. **"For many are called but, few are chosen" (Matthew 22:14).** The commandments of God will never change. Men changes the Word to what men want to hear and teach.

Many saying, "After all, my pastor went to col- lege for six years to learn to teach whatever religion he picked." Now, which denomination is better than the other? The only thing I see are those who want to change the wording to suit their way by removing what they think are old and simple words spoken by Christ and His disciples. The time is approaching where few will be chosen.

Choose the true Bible with the holy words of God that has not changed the wording when it was translated in English called the King James Bible. Remember, a **wolf in sheep's clothing is still a wolf (Matthew 7:15).** As for Satan, he is still a serpent, ready to strike even the most elect. **"For, there shall arise false Christ's and false prophets, and** shew (show) **great signs and wonders in-so-much that, if it were possible, they shall deceive even the very elect" (Matthew 24:24).**

Some of you will understand my writings, but most will not understand, and wonder where I'm coming from. This you will have to ask God to help you with.

Remember we must be subject to one another, for what you have learned will be shared with someone who sees the words differently; together we shall unite to a better understanding of what God is telling us; for a man standing alone is left ignorant.

Not everyone can teach the whole Bible, but God gave us a choice to combine our knowledge together where we can put the word and join that which we have learned from one another where we can learn the words that have come down from the beginning of time, the Bible.

What I'm trying to do is to paint a picture to where one can understand the scrolls that were handed down to us by the holy scribes. Many of the scripts (etch- ings) were found on clay slabs, some on stone, and many written-on copper scrolls and papyrus (a paper made from a tall grass that grows in the Nile), some on leather. Most of the original scrolls have withered away, with very little trace found, and many of the interpre- tations of those original scrolls that have vanished in time. With what little trace is found, the interpretations of those Scriptures will carry on by word of mouth and faith given to us by the Holy Spirit.

"The grass withers (that is, papyrus Paper), leather script, rock etchings, and flowers fade, also many of the prophets, disciples, and teachers of the Gospel. *But the word of our God stands forever"* (Isaiah 40:8-9).

This is how we received the Holy Word: through the book of God **"The Holy Bible,"** not watered-down Bibles of today that remove so many of the holy words handed down to by the prophets of the past, that were interpreted into English.

The King James Bible started in 1604 and was com- pleted in 1611. The translation was done by forty-seven scholars of different denominations who interpreted all the original manuscripts into English. The old wording may look different, but you don't have to be highly edu- cated to understand the old words, just read on and the meaning of the message comes to you through the Holy Spirit.

God is not looking for intellects, just believers. Be careful of false prophets teaching the Word to man who are lost in the new world of word-changing, where a simple word to mean something else of today's way interpreting the simple word of yesterday. Peace be with you.

Part 2

When Will the Fall of Men come?

Why do I say this? I have noticed how many people suddenly are turning to God with unknown reasons other than fear. Everyone asking for guidance and praying for God to respond right at that moment! But you, without results, wondering, "Why me, Lord?" God knows your needs, and God has a reason for His timing. Let me explain with a short story. You have a loved one who is very sick, and the doc- tors have done everything possible, but failed. Your worries are moving at a fast pace, and you, not being a believer, feel lost in wonderment, and remembering your mother talking about God that went in one ear and out the other. This leaves you wondering what to do.

The only thing left to do is to try this holy person called God; knowing that you have never depended on Him, you have taken everything for granted, but now fear and sadness has come upon you, for your most beloved one is near her end. Deep in your thoughts, you remembered what your mother tried to teach you when you were in your younger years; that with God all things are possible. Now kneeling before her bed wondering where to start, for her end is coming soon. "Where shall I start?"

You know a few people that go to church a few blocks away, but, this one is weird, and the other one is too strict and speaks a different style. By now, you are lost! A thought comes to you: what about my friend's church?   But she is a holy roller! How about Sue? But she is a Jo-ah-v!

This could go on forever, so you are now undecided. After deep thought you decided to go to the nearest church.

As you enter, you were welcomed and was asked to come forward; prayer was performed for your needs. Now time has passed with no results and you give up on God and back to your wicked ways, lost. What I'm trying to present to you with this story is that the world has been taken over by the evil one (Satan). The young man has lost the faith his mother tried to teach him and is back to where he started in a world of woe.

Folks, this is going to happen to many, and many will come seeking for God for quick answers and many will be deceived, no *not* by God, but by *Satan* who will confuse you. So, your mother has passed on, and you're now up in age and you have children of your own, you realize what you went through when you were at that age and lost. Now understanding what you went through is not an easy task to take. Sometimes it takes a lifetime before you come to know God.   Once again be careful what Bible you choose; I recommend the King James Bible; don't fall for that old saying, that it is an old English language and not used today. Just in case you don't know, the KJV is at a fifth-grade level; all other new Bibles are at an eighth grade· level and claiming that KJV is difficult is what the new scholars and today's theologies want you to believe, but the Word of God has already been interpreted and written long before any of them. Just because the scholars have a degree taught to them by another person with a degree and changing the English words with new inter- pretation of common words, like hell, now called Hades.

The word "Hades" is Greek mythology and does not appear in the King James Bible. It is hard to divide the two words. "Hades" is the word where non-believers go after death; it's not a place of torment, and some call this "limbo." What is limbo exactly? The residence of those souls excluded from heaven because of the ancient belief that it was situated near the confines to Hell, referring to the edge of hell. Basically, a spec- ulation, a theory on the afterlife and the condition of those who die whose souls were barred from heaven yet not consigned to hell on till the Day of Judgment. **"Then death and Hell were cast into the lake of fire" (Revelation 20:14).**

It is known that the words of God will never change, but the poison (power) of the serpent strikes, confusing the common people who only have maybe only an eighth' grade education if any.

The new international Bibles are replacing the Word of God by taking out and removing many words and whole verses. Look it up: **If any man shall take away from the words of this book of this prophecy, God shall add unto him the plagues written in this book (Revelation 22:19).** You cannot teach those wolves apostasy (true Christianity); so, the new religion scholars are convinced who were taught by teachers of theology who are teaching what someone else thought them, who do not open the Bible and see for themselves what they are being taught.

Of all the new Bibles out there, the NKJV (New King James Bible) is the nearest to the KJV, but I prefer to study the KJV; though the NKJV has all the verses, but, it also has many of the new wordings found in the other new Bibles that led me to believe: Am I doing right by reading the NKJB, who removes words like hell to hades, the heaven to heavens? It disturbs me to see the true and simple words from the KJV being changed to please men. A man like myself has no power to convince a preacher who has gone through college to learn the Word of God by another man who was convinced by another man that the new Bibles are right; if this is not changing the true Word of God who has been my holy teacher helping me to keep His Holy Word that has come from as far as the apostles of old who God Himself spoke with them, from Adam to Noah, on to

Moses and on to the twelve apostles of Jesus Christ.

Satan is watching every movement man make, and finds their weakest point, but with faith, God is there to save you by the blood of his only begotten Son Jesus Christ. Pray for wisdom and knowledge, your eyes will open, and you will lose the misunderstanding of who is right: man, or the words of God.

There are many out there who can quote the Bible in and out but let us go back to the apple tree; whether the apples appear red or green, when you read the Bible, you will see the words differently. Everybody has a purpose with God's interpretations, for one to teach one another.

When the apple is ripe you gathered the fruit, that is the wisdom of God and once more we share that wisdom with one another.

The Spirit of God will guide you step by step, not by the Bible-groups who can quote the Bible word for word and interpret what they think it means.

Those people can help, but it's up to your soul to listen, for God will guide you, and those who teach will be blessed. Remember this: one day your body will die, but your soul will be forever. The Lord Jesus said, ***"seek and you shall find" (Matthew 7:7)***; next: ***"I am the way and the truth and the life" (John 14:6).*** You are not alone! Enter your room, shut the door, and pray in secret to your Father; He shall reward you openly. If you can't find the words, just utter unknown words, for the Father will understand your spiritual language and what it is to have faith in what you say in prayer. **"These things we speak, not in words which man's wisdom teaches, but which the Holy Ghost teaches, comparing spiritual things with spiritual faith" (1 Corinthians 2:13).** This is between you and the Father; as for your prayers, He will keep them for- ever. It is said in **Matthew 6:5-6):** Do not be an exhibitionist when you pray in a spiritual way for all to see, do this in your closet. You don't have to prove to the world how holy you are when you talk with God Jehovah in spirit; He is the only one who will listen, and under- stand your needs, don't try to impress your parishio- ners, it may look impressing to those who know you, but you are not there to impress anyone other than **God Almighty.** God has given you the right to praise Him in your own way; this interpretation is between you and your Maker.

May the Lord richly give you peace; again, you must remember, greater is He who is in you than he who is in the world. Amen.

I firmly believe a new person who is starting his journey with God should began studying the New Testament where Jesus brings the love of men. Jesus Himself will lead you through the Old Testament; this is the law that was given to Moses at Mount Sinai with the Ten

Commandments given to men. Jesus is the way and the truth; He will not deceive you.

What does "thou shall not kill" mean **(Exodus 20:13)?** All the modern translations of the new Bibles rendered it this way: **"You shall not murder."** Murder is the unlawful and deliberate way of killing a human; to kill; to cause the death of a person, animal, or any other living creatures. God's Word, in the KJV Bible, not all killing is murder.

Murder is an unlawful crime of passion and the taking of a human life, premeditated. The command- ment not to kill, applies the taking the life of man and of animals given to us by the Highest. God gave us animals for a reason; this does not mean that humans have the right to kill or mistreat them just to show off your trophy. Again, to murder is to pre-plan to kill a human. To kill is to take the life given by God to all living things. God gave us the right to kill animals for human consumption and other needs. Killing is not for men to misuse. It is hard when one must go to war. War is for hate and power, we are forced to fight and *kill* for survival. Jesus said in **Matthew 26:52,** *"For all who draw the sword will die by the sword."*

Men today kill for pleasure, money, and power. Jesus was killed and died for our salvation and the right to live, for **God give all humans and beast a life span,** it is up to Him when our lifespan is finished here on Earth.

When looking for salvation, I recommend you start in the New Testament in **Matthew 5:17. Jesus came not to abolish the law, but to fulfill the law.** Once you have the acknowledgment why Jesus came, you can go into the Old Testament and look up the history of the past full of wars and power. The law will not get you to heaven, but the powers in His blood (Christ Jesus) will; this is His everlasting promise when He said, *"I will not leave you comfortless* (orphan), *I will come to you"* **(John 14:18).** God is the only one who has given you the knowledge called, **God's Word, the Bible.** Men have been changing many new words in the modern Bibles not spoken in biblical times. It is said, **"Who so ever shall break one of these least commandments and shall teach men so, he shall be called the least in the kingdom of heaven"** (Matthew 5:19).

I have no authority to tell you what I say is true! But you have the same God who has led me with this manuscript hoping to reach at list one person to see it in their heart to open the Bible I call the KJVB and see for yourselves. We all need someone to share the Word of God with, where we can share and help each other to understand yesterday's simple wording that has come to us through the ages.

The new wording in today's Bibles are different when using the modern words that mean so many other things not related to the King James Bible, and lead you to interpret yesterday's simple words with a different interruption.

I have been in different Bible studies when someone is using a new Bible that does not coincide with other Bibles in the room and this starts dissociation and lack of continuity between thoughts and identity as to understand what the teacher is teaching, and the teaching gets confusing.

The two Bibles I recommenced are the King James Bible and the New King James Bible. The **NKJV** though somewhat corrupted it is the closest to the KJV, so let's go from there. It's up to you to follow your faith. **"Ask and it will be given to you; seek and you shell find, knock and it will open onto you" (Matthew 7:7).** For everyone who asks, receives. Peace.

Part 3

Parables and Definitions of the Bible

The American College Encyclopedic Dictionary Very few people can interpret the Bible, and most of us take for granted what someone else has told us. What I'm about to tell you in this manuscript is my own interpretation of words that are used in the new Bibles of today that have different meaning from yesterday's way of understanding. **Now,** for you to understand what I am about to tell you, you must travel with me back in time when the scribes were the only few people that could read and write, and for them to make the common person understand the word, it had to be done in a picture-tutorial method of trans- ferring knowledge of words with frightful presentation as the serpent was, so that people could comprehend the meaning of what Satan stood for.

The people knew Satan is a fallen angel and pic- tured him as an evil subject. The symbol of a serpent or snake played important roles in religious and the cultural life of ancient Egypt and Greece. To them "ser- pent" represented a symbol of evil from the underworld of Satan. The scribes had to show how frightful this evil spirit the devil really is, so, for the scribes to picture how dreadful this demon called Satan was, they had to show fear with the only symbol or sign for under- standing between good and evil; back then the serpent was the most feared of all creature, for the serpent strikes when least excepted as Satan does also, for the serpent, or snake, has been associated with some of the oldest rituals known to humankind and represents dual expression of good and evil. Serpent, the name given to a snake in a religious context, said to have tempted Adam and Eve in the Garden of Eden. Read carefully the next paragraph.

Here are the true serpents and true scorpions to which Christ is referring. **"The unclean spirits and demons with false doctrines."** Let me start with **Mark 16:17/18**: **"Those who believe in my name shall cast out demons." (that is devils). "They shall take up serpents" (meaning, removal of unclean spirits, demons, not picking up a poisonous snake), and if they drink any deadly thing, (that is to take in, or absorb sinful ways, not poison) if they con- fess openly to God it will not hurt them; they will recover and be free from sin. They shall lay hands on the sick and they will recover. This could not be plainer:** do not tempt God by taking poison as the **NIV proclaims,** by saying **Mark 16:18**: **"They will pick up snakes; with their hands; and when they drink deadly poison, it will not hurt them at all."** This is not what Jesus is telling you; those two deceiving words, **snake and poison**, will kill you, and so **"will sin."** Who are those, **they,** that the NIV is speaking of? Now look up **Luke 10:19. "Behold I give you power** (the authority) **to trample on serpents and scor- pions (meaning satanic spirit, followers of Satan), and over all the power of the enemy and nothing shall by any means hurt you."** Remember **snakes** and **serpents** won't send you to **hell,** but the **sins** of the devil will. **To understand** the Word means having faith (truth). Though you may not have much knowl- edge of the Bible, the spirit within you and your will- power is all you need, let God do the rest. In Him (God) you can trust. Let not your heart be troubled, so says the Lord. So be it.

Spiritualizing Scripture Words of the Bible

Serpent: meaning a treacherous spirit as Satan, who places the poison of asps (**sin**) under the lips of sinners, tempting to destroy their soul with sin
   Demons: are unclean satanic spirits.
   Scorpion: Meaning demons, which afflict sin as the pain of a scorpion's sting. A sinful spiritual death waits.

Deadly: A deadly word that poisons and corrupts the mind, aiming to kill or destroy your faith.

Poison: To ruin, or vitiate making, one weak with sin; corrupting the mind with drinks and drugs that destroy body and soul.

Drink: Meaning to absorb, to take in, and accepting sinful ways.

Enemy: one involved in a spiritual death, a satanic deceiver of the word of God. (Satan).

Don't just take those seven words for what you think they mean. We are now seeking what the Lord is telling us, that with faith you shall seek, and you will understand what salvation truly mean by seeking the true meaning of those seven words used in the Scriptures of yesterday handed down to us by our fore- fathers and their forefathers. How many of you have ever tried to pick up a snake or a scorpion, thinking it will not hurt you because you are full of the Holy Spirit? There are many who try to interrupt the biblical words without understanding that in those days, very few people could read or interrupt what Christ truly meant; for only a fool would tempt to pick up one of those poisonous critters just to prove their misunder-standing of how holy they think they are, playing with temptation that God never intended to test men with. Many don't realize or understand what the scribes are talking about when using those words. Those seven words refer to Satan's distraction of men. **"The thief comes not, but for to steal and to kill and to, destroy" (John 10:10).** Next, **Revelation 12:9. "So, the great dragon was cast out, that serpent of old, called the Devil and Satan who deceives the whole world."** He was cast to earth with his angels involving spiritual death (a deadly sin). **Revelation 12:12** says, **"Woe to the inhabitants of the earth and the sea, for the Devil has come having great wrath."** I employ you to study the Bible, **not** with modern word Bibles, just plain English found in the KJV. I prefer you study the King Janes Bible and go from there. Forget these modern so-called Bibles like the NIV; even this pas- sage in Revelation 12:12 is incomplete; the wording is incorrect. Look this up yourself. The KJV and the NKJV says, **"Woe to the *inhabitants* of the earth and the sea."** The NIV says, **"But,**

woe to the earth." God is not judging the earth; the earth is a place, **inhabitants are those who dwell or occupant therein.**

Be not deceived by new wording. I am sure many will disagree, but, many of you will understand and see the difference; just believe in the Lord Jesus Christ whose blood paid the debt for our sins committed.

"For if we die with him, we shall also live with him; if we suffer, we shall reign with him: if we deny him, he also will deny us. For a soul not repenting will shall surely die" (2 Timothy 2:12). "For the words of the Lord are pure words" (Psalm 12:6). Truth. Believe, and Jesus will lead you correctly, for God has given man an instruction manual called **The Holy Bible** to follow.

Be careful with the door to distraction, for it is widely open where riches and sin can make you blind; seek for faith and godly riches untold, this you can take with you all the days of your eternal life in heaven. Jesus said, *"For the day is coming when many shall come saying that I am the Christ, and shells deceive many"* (Matthew 24:5).

About 1980 or so, a new tern came about the KJB, with claims the holy books of the original arrangement is incorrect; so, the ecumenical council gathered to discuss how to remove the KJV and replace it with the New Age movement Bibles. If you look back earlier, I named several of the new interpretations of the Bible by Harper Collins, a Zondervan publication, owned by Rupert Murdoch, known for their erratic porn books, and **satanic** evil books. **Zondervan own the copyrights to the NIV Bible, and many other new Bibles; tragically Murdoch bought out the Thomas Nelson publications. The KJV Bible has no copy- rights.** Murdoch is in it for the money. To him, the KJV is just another money-making book. **Once again,**

1 Corinthians 10:21: "You cannot drink the cup of the Lord and the cup of the demons." You must pick one. If it wasn't for those who oppose the KJV, those new Bibles would not exist, wanting to destroy and to put an end and demolishing the word therein.

A large group at the ecumenical counsel of Rome, and many religious groups, gathered in the Vatican coming together to discuss how to omit the KJV from true believers saying the wording is outdated and to omit many of the verses that have been with the original transitions of the original tongues. How then? Bibles like the NIV (mostly used) omit so many verses that Jesus spoke to us, **marked in red,** that were replaced by a group of men and women who seem to be saying that the words of Jesus are not important enough to print in their new Bibles. If this is not an antichrist revision, then you tell me.

A large majority of the new Bibles are published by News Corp., a Rupert Murdoch publication well known for his erratic and pornographic publications, and owner of the exclusive printing copyrights to the NIV, who is owned by the Zondervan publishers; if you remember he also publishes the **Satanic Bible** and **witchcraft books**, tragically. Murdoch also owns the **FOX** news media, with cartoons like "Family Guy", full of filth not suitable for children, and disrespect. What about "South Park" and "The Simpsons" represents the children of today? Watching so-called adult entertain- ment in a cartoon presentation; this is the door of diffu- sion spreading widely to the future of our youth. As for Mama and Papa, they are working, and the babysitter doesn't care, for she is enjoying the TV along with the small children.

Many large radio stations do voice operations where many so-called famous televangelists deceive many, saying how much God loves you, and living high on the hog, and asking for more money as the Pharisees and the Sadducees did; this you can find in the internet. I'm not making any of this up. All this is about the **New World Movement** mentioned in the Bible in **Luke**

12:53: There will be division in the church, father against son, mother against daughter, and so forth.

Many of you don't like to be told about what harm those things I am talking about are doing to the chil- dren who know more than I did when I was twenty. Now, learn what the new modern Bibles are doing to you by changing the wording now replaced by men. Modern wording will not save you; these new books only tell you part of the Scriptures that some modern theologian who thinks that he knows more than the Scribes of the past that witnessed the commandments that God spoke to his servants.

Those new books are duping you with many words that supposedly sound good yet mean something dif- ferent. By looking at those new books (Bibles) they should be smaller after the removal of the many verses from the KJB, but as you can see, the reason they are so large is because of the many footnotes trying to convince you how the words of God are not important enough in the KJV and omitting many verses spoken by the apostles, and Jesus Himself. I'm not saying for you not to read those so-called Bibles; many have said how they were saved by these books, no, not by the book, but by the Holy Spirit that is leading you; now open your eyes, a new world awaits you when you look up the wordings in the KJV.

Please, consider the KJV vs. the NIV on the NET.

You will see how the world is turning around the true word of God. Again, **"Take heed that no man deceives you, "For many shall in my name come saying, I am Christ; and shall deceive many" (Matthew 24:4-5).**

I feel the time is now approaching when the prin- cipality against the flash and blood are turning to the power of Satan's wicked spirits. It is easy to say, "I'm saved," but are you? Not when you are missing the true words of God's instruction manual (the Bible) that Jesus spoke to His disciples, including you and me. Even the most elite (privileged people) will be deceived by all those new way Bibles.

Now, go read **Mark 13:21-22** and listen what He said, **"And if any man shall say to you, Lo, here is Christ; or lo, he is there; believe him not for false Christs and false prophets shall rise, and shall shew** (show) **signs and wonders, to seduce, if it were pos- sible, even the elect."** I'm not asking for you to do what I say, just consider what I'm trying to show you. Go look for yourselves on YouTube: KJV vs. NIV. I'm but a voice who is seeking the truth in God.

The best-selling Bible today is the so-called NIV that has taken away the words "God" and "Jesus" dozens of times and so many verses removed; the word "hell" has been replaced with the word Hades, a Greek word.

The word "hades" does not appear in the King James Version of the Bible. In the days of Jesus when He was here on Earth, many were killed for speaking out His teachings; today many are laughing at you for speaking the truth. **What is truth?** This you should look up for yourselves, what is true for me may not be truth for you.

Remember the Lord God has His arms open; seek and you shall (will) find. **"So, faith comes from hearing, and hearing by the word of God (Romans 10:17).** Not by the books and copyrights by owners like Rupert Murdoch who is in it for the money, evil or good, he doesn't care.

The King James Bible has no copyrights as the new Bibles of today have, and you cannot use or change any of their wordings. The KJV is there for your knowledge and salvation. Seek and you shall find the truth that comes by faith. Take heed, the time is at hand when confession and misunderstanding will confuse you; be not deceived by false doctoring, listen to your spirit, and be careful of him (Satan) who is in the world, even in the most Holy places one can imagine, and who has great power, more than you will ever endeavor. But your heart has the **Holy Spirit** listen to it wisely and with faith you shall be free.

Salvation comes through faith and grace alone. May the Lord God Jehovah, Jesus Christ our Lord, or the Holy Ghost (Spirit), no matter by which way you call Him, know this, **"From everlasting to ever ever- lasting, thou art God" (Palm 90:2).** Let's go on.

The word "**God head**": This phrase has been removed from the new Bibles, found only in the KJB. Many theologians say all Bible versions are basically the same and that the only difference is just minor wording changes—not so. Therefore, I have taken the time with hope in showing you as to what I and many other Christians see as to what is happening in the days to come. Not only what you see or hear, but the very words in the new Scriptures that are trying to wipe out my believing in the 1611 translations. A language or tongue that has been passed on to me and you by our forefathers, before we became so intellectual and started changing common words to a new way of inter- pretations of those very words I have heard all my life; the same language since their arrival in 1776 when my parents' families landed (arrived) here in America. Beware! A new wave of viperous (antichrist) who are trying to replace the very words of God, with new word Bibles of today that mean differently and changing the meaning of His word by removing and replacing with men's interpretation. For instance, the sixth com- mandment, "Thou shall not kill", is being replaced with, "You shall not murder": two different meanings.

I'm not saying those men don't believe, but men don't have the right to change yesterday's words to suit their interpretation, just to sell their books.

The KJV is simple to understand, it's a fifth-grade level Bible. Don't change the meanings of the holy words passed on to us by the men who God selected to hand us the law. God has sent His only begotten son Jesus Christ to teach us and to give us **our instruction manual** called The Holy Bible. I am a KJV believer; hopefully you will consider what I and many other Christians have come to believe, in a Bible without copyrights. The new Bibles of today that have copyrights that don't allow anyone to change the wording, unlike the KJB. Beware of sheep in wolves' clothing, for at night all sheep are black, and you may not be able to distinguish the differences and take the misunderstanding of the new way Bibles that are missing so many **words** and **verses** therein.

Jesus said, ***"I am the light of the world: he that follows me shall not walk in darkness but shall have the light of life"*** **(John 8:12).** You don't have to take my word; this I will leave that up to God and you. Just say; **"I need you Lord, my amazing grace."**

Part 4

Be Still and Know That I Am God.

(Psalm 46:10)

Faith

What is faith? Having faith will lead you to salvation, hope, and belief that Jesus is the way, the truth, and the life. Jesus is "love" **(John 14:6).**

Remove a mountain? What does this mean? Jesus, going into the city of Bethany, felt hunger; he saw a fig tree and walking up to the tree, found no fruit among its leaves, so Jesus ordered the tree to wither away, no more to produce. Jesus was asked why. Jesus said, ***"Verily (truly) I say to you, if you have faith and doubt not, you shall not only do as I did, and if you say to that mountain to be removed and be cast to the sea, and you truly have faith it shall be done; what so ever you ask in prayer, believing and you shall receive"*** **(Matthew 21:21).** This is my interpretation.

Once again let's go back to the time of Jesus, pre- AD. This is the way I interpret this parable. "To remove a mountain?" What is meant to remove a mountain? Knowing my faith is of man and it is weak, the only way I can remove a mountain is with the intelligence the Lord has given me; that is to take a tractor and a truck and started moving dirt, **but**, this is not what Jesus is talking about; He is talking about the faith of removing a big problem (sin) that can be replaced (removed) by prayer and faith; no man has the power to move the earth about as Jesus did, but the fig tree was a way to symbolize (show) to them, **the apostles,** that by prayer obstacles and things can be removed just as the fig tree that represented an obstacle (a barrier) that blocked a necessity to continue with their journey.

One way to look at this is, when you meet someone who does not want to hear you talk about helping them with the word of salvation, rebuke thy self and walk away; you were not welcome, just as Jesus did when He walked away from the fig tree.

The fig tree was an obstacle; Jesus did not remove it because it was in the way, no, this was a way to show the power they the apostle had if they only use their faith. Let's look at the book of Matthew. **"And who- soever shall not receive you, nor hear your words, ye depart out of that house or city, and shake the dust from your feet, and walk away, you were not received" (Matthew 10:14).**

Many of you take words literally as you see them, but, do you understand the message or the interpreta- tion to where it will make sense? I myself don't believe anyone has ever moved a real mountain— no, only Jesus is capable of that. Though, when you pray for someone you love or something that needs dire assis- tance, try praying, have faith. These are mountains you and I can truly move. Jesus said, *"And all things, whatsoever you ask in prayer, believing, and you shall receive."* **(Matthew 21:22).** In no way can a man move a mountain here on Earth by saying "remove thy self," but you can remove a mountain of sorrow that surrounds your life, whether with you or with your loved ones by accepting the power of prayer and under- standing what Jesus truly meant when He (Jesus) said, **"You can move a mountain."**

This was a way of expressing the power the apostles had received, by believing and prayer they could heal those with infirmities, and evil satanic spirits. Again, only Jesus can remove real mountains, but He has given us the power to remove the mountains of sorrow, that is, sin and disgrace from those who need healing and salvation. Again, as far as I know, I know not, nor heard of anyone who has ever moved a real mountain, but I have witnessed many healings by prayer, rep- resenting a mountain of sorrow to many. Reminder: this is the way that I interpret the parable to where hopefully you will understand what it means to remove a mountain. Jesus is the only one who can open your eyes so that you may be able help someone else to understand what is meant to remove a mountain. I'm not here to change the Bible, just to help you to under- stand what God has given me, where I can remove a mountain of sorrow and infirmity from those who need healing and prayer.

Praise God.

Part 5

The Battle of Man and Spirit Begins

Before the time of Noah's life, it was Adam's world. How old was Adam at his end? The Bible, according to the gospel, says he lived to be 930 years; he had many sons and daughters as the world multi- plied. There was an 1,100-year gap between Adam and the birth of Noah (around ten generations). Adam died 216 years before the birth of Noah. Seth was Adam's third son, who lived 912 years; Seth knew Noah for thirty-four years before he died. Methuselah was the fourth grandson of Seth, who lived 969 years; it is said that Methuselah is the oldest man who ever lived; he died in the year of the flood in 1656 AM (*Anno Mundi*).

As the world advanced and grew larger, men had become knowledgeable and worldly and became so disagreeable with one another and started to walk in sin.

Sin of hate became a way of life siding with Satan's evil direction, making sin desirable and adventurous.

Man became deaf and blind to the Word of God. Satan's ways were so convincing even some of the angels had distanced away from God and united with Lucifer (the fallen angel). **"How art thou fallen from heaven O Lucifer, son of the morning, which didst weaken the nations!" (Isaiah 14:12).**

Lucifer is only mentioned once in the KJV (now referred to as Satan). The word Lucifer is not men- tioned in any other Bible, only in the King James Bible that I know of. The world became satanic and sided with the evil one, Satan, the keeper of the bottomless pit, who also became the evil spirit of the air. **And there was a war in heaven: Michael and his angels fought against the dragon (Revelation 12:7).**

After the Great War in heaven, the great dragon Lucifer was cast out from heaven with one-third of the angels and was sent down to Earth. Unknown what the earth was like after Adam sinned; we cannot even come close to a vision of that time before the flood. The world became adulterous, filled with sin and sodomite, man with man and woman with woman alike.

What about the children? Never mentioned therein? They also must have been involved with much sin and disobedient with a world gone badly.

The children of today are becoming rude and dis- respectful, that recalls an unproven fact of what the children of Noah's days were like; did they have a disre- spectful behavior? Which is one of the improper way's kids behave today, especially teenagers, trying to solve problems amongst themselves. What does the Bible say? **For which things shake the wrath of God cometh on the children of disobedience (Colossians 3:6).**

Teachers today are not held in the same regard as they once were by children or parents. A child of twelve today knows more than we did at the age of twenty. The

1960s children have had the best teacher ever, the tele- vision, full of so much disobedient and sexual activities, and knowledge that we so-called Christians overlook; we worry more about the abortion than the root as to where it starts.

Since the late 1960s, the movies have been the teacher for little children on having sex; there's not a movie no matter how good you think it is that doesn't have an excerpt (lesson) on sex. They never leave out the sex plot or the vulgar language. This is a mon- ey-making business, and no one cares how it is made, and most people of today have approved of it. Now, you tell me which **sin comes first? How to have sex, or, the abortion** that comes from ignorance thereafter? Hypocrite, sin starts at the beginning, once it is done, it can't be undone; shame makes one killer of the unborn, saying "not my child," or a man who doesn't care and lies how much he loves her, and you girls are so gull- ible. Don't pretend you don't know what you are doing.

Life is not a make-believe world. Back in the Vietnam War, we, the voters, passed the law to let the eigh- teen-year-old vote because they were of draft age. This was the **biggest** mistake we have ever made; this is the time when an eighteen-year-old just out of school is just finding out what it is to become an adult, a time to grow up and take responsibility and how to sur- vive without Mama and Papa. The eighteen-year-old became the majority, and out-voted the elders, and created new laws, just because we felt sorry for them going to war. When you are in the military you learn how to survive, you become a responsible adult. War is hell; I don't wish this on anyone.

You know that in an election the majority wins; that so happened with our eighteen-year-olds; we were so gullible and forgot how large the population of young- sters had become and outvoted their lovable parents three to one. The rule became, "I got my rights; I'm eighteen now and I'm out of here." Leaving their par- ents brokenhearted for the laws were changed to suit them. You hypocrites protest on abortion but not *the source* where it all starts! **Your television, and sub- jective movies**, where is your protest now? And your schools where kids gather wanting to be sexy just to become poplar.

We have made rules that will prohibit teachers to dis- cipline your children. You will march on abortion how bad it is, but no one will march on the **TV networks or movies** that influence your kids with sexual and vulgarity motivations just because it's entertainment.

Looking back at the seventies, TV began the "Three is Company" series, where the teenagers learned to live on their own in mixed company, sexually motivated, inappropriate. PG movies are a joke; I guess it is meant for forty-year old teenagers. As for TV and radio, you women will miss "As the World Turns", not to forget "The Young and Restless", full of inappropriate samples of how we should live life.

Look at your home life with your kids, look at their cell phone; they don't need you to get advice. You are too dumb and outdated and now the rappers become the messengers and influential in a musical form kids relate to. Quit looking at your selfish religious glory and talk with God to show you how to fulfill His spirit in your heart and regain power over your children.

Teach your children about the fact of life; don't depend on the school or cell phones. Kids are intelli- gent, but they don't know which way to go: with Christ or Satan! It's up to you to teach them. The kids know, but they don't want their friends to think how square they are when they pick Jesus. The only home the kids know today is, "The House of Fear" where the older street gang members become their authority.

Parents become blinded and afraid to punish their kids. Who made the changes in the laws of today when they received the right to vote at eighteen? Don't tell me "not my kids" when both parents are not around, the **cell phone** becomes their parents. Kids are looking for fun without a responsibility. What a father or mother don't know when looking at their innocent faces, is it right or wrong? These, I will leave up to you. May the Lord forgive us and led us in the right direction.

Part 6

Turning to Please Men

Again, no one knows what the world was like at the time of Noah. Was it beyond our comprehen- sion as we know it today? I believe we are going in that direction; **even the church is turning to please man**, not by grace of God. Once again, I repeat: stay away from the so-called new Bibles that only teach half of the word therein and omit the **truth** by leaving out so many verses handed down to us by the disciples that Jesus was teaching the true inspirational Word of God. I know, I wasn't there, but neither were you. Man's confusion has taken us by misinterpretation of the simple words that the Lord was teaching, so one could comprehend His words and bring His word to others with less intellect. But, man today have become so knowledgeable, and linguist thinking that the dis- ciple's simple writings need to be changed into higher form of new English; so, man began writing what they thought was simple and modern changing to what our Lord had said in the simplest way. **Jesus did not come to teach new words of confusion; His words are pure and simple.** The "thee" and the "thou" are simple words; if you have studied English in school and read Shakespeare and other books, you should understand the KJV, but that's not what it is; you just don't want to read the King James Bible because someone told us it was outdated and too hard to read. My friends, I'm not trying to force you to change your Bible; just com- pare them side by side. This is the only way you see what changes man have made, by removing words with new words that could mean something so differently.

All those new Bible changes came about in the late

1950s. I cannot believe that even Baptist churches are changing to the NIV. These were strict KJV churches when I was a young man, but evil can change even the most elect. All they have to say is, "I know the Word of God better than the disciples of time passed." God forbids. I have been a Christian all my life and it has taken me a long time to understand the Holy Word. I am eighty-six and the Lord has opened my mind not with religion, but with Christianity.

I have visited many religious groups telling me their way is the only way to salvation and that all the other religious groups are wrong. It is hard for me to believe the separation there is in God's Word (the church). The time has come for us to unite together with the Word (the Bible). It is man and his selfish beliefs who won't unite because he or she was taught by great scholars of theologue who have interpreted the word of Christ to their own interpretation changing the words to their way of believing.

Together we can put the Word into an understanding with one another, no matter what church you attend. There will be many harsh words said when debating; take a deep breath and listen to one another; the Spirit of the Lord will be there with you.

Praise God. **For God, did not send His Son into the world to condemn the world; but that the world through Him might be saved (John 3:17).**

Part 7

Let's move on, God's Word, the Bible.

King James Version Vs New International Version (NIV)

KJB began Genesis Chapter 1: "In the beginning God created **heaven and the earth**." The new Bibles of today (the NIV, ASV, NASV, AMP, RSV, NLT, ESV, CEV, NKJB) all have changed the wording to say, "in the beginning, God created the heavens," meaning more than one.

In days of time passed, man did not have schooling as we do now, so, "Heavens" was used to separate the steps of the whole universe. Paul and other apostles in the Bible, to make people understand, separated heaven into three parts and called them "heavens," referring to the firmament separation in the universe, that indicates the whole universe. Usually: the three heavens are divided as follows. The first Heaven: our immediate atmosphere holding carbon dioxide (C02) that surrounds and sustains life and the very air we breathe, and a place where birds fly. The second Heaven is, the stellar heaven, outer space, where the sun, planets, and the moon are placed. God knew men would one day travel beyond the stellar heaven, trying to prove His existences in His celestial Heaven. The so-called third heaven represents the special place where God of the Bible resides: the home of God. All this can be found in many chapters in the KJV Bible. We need to hold on to our declaration of faith; **if God says Heaven, accept what God said.**

His presence is everywhere in the universe He calls **Heaven**. **Prerace the Lord.** Now let's go on with the interpretation of the KJV vs. the NIV. Let's start with:

KJV–Luke 9:56: "For the Son of man is not come to destroy man's live, but to save them. And they went to another village."

NIV–Luke 9:56: "and they went to another village"

KJV–Matthew 18:11: "For the Son of man is come to save that which is lost" NIV–Matthew 18:11–Missing

KJV- Matthew 9:13: "I am not come to call the righ- teous, but sinners to repentance."

NIV–Matthew 9:13: "I have not come to call the rightness, but sinners."

KJV- 1 Corinthians 5:7: "Christ our Passover is sacrificed for us:"

NIV–1 Corinthians 5:7: "Christ our Passover lamb, has been sacrificed."

JKV- John 6:47: "Verily, verily (truly, truly) I say unto you, He that believeth on me hath everlasting life." NIV–John 6:47: "I tell you the truth, he who believes has everlasting life." *("He who believes"? Believes in what? This line is incomplete.)*

KJV–Luke 2:33: "And Joseph and his mother mar- veled at those things which were spoken of him."

NIV–Luke 2:33: "The child's father and his mother marveled at what was said about him." *(God is the Father of Jesus, Joseph was Jesus' guardian and never claimed the state of being the father of Jesus.)*

KJV–Mark 3:15: "Power to heal sickness, and to cast out devils"

NIV–Mark 3:15: "Authority to drive out demons." *(Many of us think those two terms are one and the same, but there exists a fine line of difference with power and authority. Power given by God. Authority given by man.)*

KJV–Mark 11:26: "But if you do not forgive, nei- ther will your Father which in heaven forgiven your trespasses."

NIV–Mark 11:26 (missing)

KJV- 1 Corinthians 10:28: "for the earth is the Lord's fullness thereof"

NIV -1 Corinthians 10:28: "for the earth is the Lords." The *last part of the verse is missing* (fullness thereof).

KJV- Matthew 5:44: "Love your enemies, bless them

that curse you, do good to them that hate you, and pray for them which despitefully use you, and per- secute you."

NIV–Matthew 5:44: "Love your enemies pray for those who persecute you."

KJV–John 16:16: "A little while, and ye shall not see me: and again, a little while, and ye shall see me, because I go see my Father."

NIV–John 16:16: "In a little while you will see me on more, and then after a little while you will see me." *(This wording is unbelievable: "you will see me no more!")*

This is not what John wrote. The correct punctua- tions are missing, thus the NIV is incorrect.

When an upcoming Christian is forced to look up foot- notes to try to comprehend the footnotes he or she is looking at, they will assume it to be right to what man has replaced from the true Word of God and become confused.

The **NIV** also removes words along with the "thee", "thou", "thou shall not" for a grand total of over **64,575 omissions**.

Here are a few of the omissions: "Christ" is removed 25 times "Lord" is removed 350 times "Jesus" is removed over 290 times "God" is removed 460 times "Godhead" is removed 3 times

"Lucifer" is removed only one time that the NIV men- tions and refers to Satan as, "The Star of the morning," **the same as Christ is described in Revelation 22:16** (the interpretation is different, Isaiah 14:12 and Revelation 22:16)

"Devil" or "demons" is removed 80 times

"Hell" is removed 40 times

"Heaven" is removed 160 times

"Damned" (or a variation) is removed 15 times

"Blood" is removed 41 times

"Salvation" is removed 42 times

"The word of God" is removed 8 times

"The Word of the Lord" is removed 24 times, and

"The Lord Jesus Christ" is removed 24 times.

The Sixth Commandment, "Thou shall not kill," is replaced with, "You shall not murder." Why the NIV and the likes have removed the words of the KJV is unknown, those words are pure, and part of the interpretations handed down to us and translated to common English, so that common folks could read and understand. The modern English of today has changed the words to mean more than one thing, and this becomes misleading to the true understanding of the words and verses that have come down to us therein.

You must know what the Word of God is saying before you remove or replace any words; I cannot make this any plainer, other than publishers keeping their copyrights on their new word Bibles. **The words of the Lord are pure words: Thou shall keep them, O lord, thou shall preserve them from this generation for- ever" (Psalm 12:7).**

These two verses are very important to me, as they will be for you. **"For I testify unto every man that hearth the words of the prophecy of this book, if any man shall add unto this thing, God shall add unto him the plagues that are written in this book" (Revelation 22:18). "And if any man shall take away from the words of this prophecy, God shall take away his part out the 'book of life,' and out of the holy city, and from the things which are written in this book" (Revelation 22:19).**

The NIV calls **"the book of life"**, **"*the tree of life.*"** Two different meanings: the tree of life is in the midst (center) of the Garden of Eden; the book of life is in the hands of our Lord Jesus Christ; you don't write on a tree trunk. In the book of life, your name is scribed in the archive of God. The Bible tells us, **"He that hath an ear, let's hear what the Spirit said unto the churches; To him that overcome will I give to eat of the tree of life, which is in the midst of the par- adise of God" (Revelation 2:7). "And I saw the dead small and great, stand before God; and the books were opened. and another book was opened: which is The Book of Life" (Revelation 20:12).** Again, the **tree of life is not the book of life.** Those are but a few verses to show the difference between a man Bible the NIV (New International Version) and the KJV (The King James Version) handed down to us by our forefathers.

It is up to you, which road you take. Removing over

64,575 words from the book that has been handed down to us from the day our forefathers landed on American soil, and now we are told that the Word of God in this archive are too complex and cannot be understood? If you don't place them (the Bibles) side by side, you will not know the true words handed down to us by the holy scribes who were selected disciples chosen by God.

Who are these people who are convincing so many that the KJV is incorrect by replacing so many words and using footnotes to convince that the KJV is not right in their eyes? This I will leave up to you, for the Holy Spirit will guide you. **So, then faith comes from hearing by the word of God (Romans 10:17).**

Jesus said, onto them. ***"Well, hath Isaiah prophe- sied of you hypocrites, as it is written, this people honor me with their lips, but their heart is far from me. How be it, and in vain they worship me, teaching for doctrines the commandments of men. For laying aside the commandment of God"*** **(Mark 7:6-8).** I am not asking you to drink from the cup that I drink from, but if you thirst, take this cup given to me by grace, drink of it; it will open your eyes.   Now going back to the time of Noah. Wickedness began to multiply on the face of the earth. The Lord saw that the wackiness of man was great, and God was sorry that He had made man. God grieved deep in his heart for both man, beast, and the birds of the air, for they had become disobedient. God said, ***"I am sorry I have made them, I will destroy man whom I have cre- ated"*** **(Genesis 6:6).**

The creation of man and beast had become so cor- rupt before God, and it grieved his heart. Filled with vio- lence and disobedience, the Lord said, ***"I will destroy man whom I have created from the face of the earth, both man and beast and all creeping things, and the fowls of the air; for it repenteth me that***

I have made them" **(Genesis 6:7).** But in the eyes of God one man called Noah, a just man that walked and pleased God, God saw the goodness in Noah and said to Noah, ***"The end of all flesh has come before me, for the earth is filled with violence through them; and behold I will destroy them with the earth."*** With inspiration, God said to Noah, ***"Be behold your faith, you will make yourself an ark***

out of gopherwood and pitch, 3 level high rooms shalt thou make in the ark" **(Genesis 6:13).** Noah was given the measure- ments; he obeyed God's command. Noah was 600 years old when he entered the ark. He took two of every beast and birds with him and his family. The moment of the flood was at hand. It took Noah and his family approx- imately 370 days before he walked on land once again. So, God blessed Noah and his sons and said to them, ***"Go forth and be fruitful and multiply and fill the earth"*** **(Genesis 9:1).** From that time Noah and his family lived from what the earth supplied them with, and from what they cultivated from the animals that were for meat and their fur and the crops they grew.

Unknown to us what it was like before the flood, and the way things are going today, maybe one day we will able to go back and forth wherever we want to go here on Earth, by just saying, "This is Captain Kirk, from the Enterprise, beam me up Scotty." Heaven forbids. Low and behold, it is Jesus who will give us the honor of beaming us to our celestial home. Jesus said, ***"Let not your heart be troubled: ye believe in God believe also in me; and if I go and prepare a place for you, I will come again, and receive you unto myself; that where I am, ye may be also.*** **(John 14:1-3).**

This is the way the truth, and life. Amen.

Part 8

Who is Killing the King James Bible?

The KJV came about in the year 1604/1611. King James selected fifty-four men of different denominations to interpret the Hebrew, Greek, and the Latin wording of the set manuscripts that came through the generations per the disciples of that time. It took over seven years to come up with the KJVB. This is the Bible that came with the settlers to the American colonies around 1690/1692, before the pil- grims became settled. Nothing was changed in the KJV and it is still basic as it was written in 1611; as far as I know.

The biggest change came about in the 1950s when the Harper Collins Corruptions and Margit Ingram Corporations took all the copyrights to all the Bibles. Zondervan is a subsidiary of Harper Collins pub- lishing, which is owned by News Corp, owned by Robert Murdoch who now owns Thomas Nelson. Murdoch is one of the biggest producers of worldwide pornography on the planet, and his company, Zondervan, holds the exclusive publishing rights to the **New International Version** Bible. His most famous book sellers are the NIV Bible, the Satanic Bible, Witchcraft book, and of course his famous *Playgirl* magazines of all types. If you have read my script, you know the history of how so misinformed all those new Bibles are, and, supposed to be easy to read, but they are just stories claiming to be the Holy Bible, confusing the public and claiming by saying the KJV is too hard to read, yet, the new Bibles are using words that can mean something different and can confuse many; they are just money makers for Robert Murdoch. So, who are the most foolish: those who omit the KJV, who leave out so many words and full verses as the NIV and all the new so-called Bibles?

I say again, look for yourself. This is simple go on the internet and look up "KJV vs. the NIV" and there you will see the harm you will fall into by looking down at me and other Christians whose eyes have been opened by The Holy Spirit, who lets us translate the holy Word of The King James Bible. Friends, I'm not saying for you not to read those books, or saying you are wrong, but seek and you will find the truth in a Bible that has not removed words and full verses spoken by our Lord Jesus and His disciples. Again, I say, seek and you shall find, ask and you will be given, knock and it will be open for you. Jesus said, ***"Love your enemies, and pray for them which despitefully use you, and persecute you"*** **(Matthew 5:44).** This you must pray every day, for it is most unforgiven from the beginning of time when the Serpent (Satan) said to Eve in the garden, **"Ye shall not surely not die" (Genesis 3:4).** Next go to **Matthew 7:22-23:** ***"For many will say to me that day Lord, Lord have we not prophesied in your name."*** Jesus profess unto them, ***"I never knew: depart from me, ye that work iniquity."*** Now know this, for **"many are called but few are chosen."**

What is truth? It is the Word of God. From the beginning of time, God has spoken the truth; He who loved the world so, that He sent His only begotten Son to suffer and died for our sinful ways, just so you and I can have life everlasting in His kingdom and that your name be placed in the Book of Life.

To those who say, "I'm saved," yet, you find it hard to love and forgive those who go against your way of believing, I am not here to change your ways. I know it must be hard to hear what hurts your way of believing, but that is not why I wrote this ledger, and I don't have the right to try to change your way of believing, I just want to share what I have found, and I feel the Holy Spirit has opened my eyes, and I want you to share the Holy Scriptures that I and many other Christians have come to believe. I speak from the heart and share my thoughts with you. May the Lord richly bless you.

Part 9

Where Do We Go from Here?

"Where do we go from here?" How many times have I heard this? And I'm sure you have also. In the beginning, God gave man everything man needed; He loved us so much that He gave us free will and all He asked from us is to love Him and obey and appreciate the life given to us. Now, let's look at Revelation 12.

War started in heaven with Lucifer and the Archangel Michel. Lucifer, who God gave great power, wanted to exalt himself above God. Let us go on!

Revelation 12:3: And there appeared another wonder in heaven; and behold a great red dragon (the Devil).

Revelation 12:4: and his tail drew one third part of the stars of heaven, (falling angels), **and did cast them to the earth (Revelation 12:7). And there was war in heaven: Michel and his angels fought against the dragon** (Satan) **(Revelation 12:9).**

And the great dragon was cast out, that old Serpent, called the Devil, and Satan, which deceiveth the whole world: he was cast out onto the earth, and his angels were cast out with him (Revelation 12:13). And when the dragon saw that he was cast unto the earth, he persecuted the woman who brought forth the man-child which keep the commandment of God and have the testi- mony of Jesus Christ, given to us.

Men has not learned as they go on looking for answers in other so-called Bible that miss so many verses thinking the KJV is not important enough and should be replaced. Why is man so afraid of the KJB? They blame it on the old English, what a poor excuse. Men believe more on what men have interpret than the words of the apostles of time passed who, many of them have written their biography of that time, and who many did walk with Jesus.

Again, I'm not telling you what to do; just consider what I see, and what the world is coming to. We are becoming a world of science fiction coming true. I still believe all this is a repeat of the time before Noah. Just a theory deep in my mind and the possibility of a lost civilization unknown to us, for God left little trace of the time before Noah. **Jesus said, "*But! as the days of Noah were, so shall also the coming of the Son-of man be.*" (Matthew 24:37, 39).** Take a good look at this passage. I know that I keep repeating this farce, but it is the only clue Jesus has given us what is to come.

It had to be Noah who brought the first history of the evaluation of God followed by the first book of Mosses called Genesis (the creation); just look at the way things that are going on today. All we have is fear of the unknown, so men go to outer space looking for God and answers, and all that men have found are answers man cannot comprehend or understand. That it is a universe without end that He, God, called Heaven. When the time comes, God will reveal His glory to all, big and small. From everlasting to everlasting, thou art God. Praise God.

Part 10

Why Did Jesus Come to Earth?

Christians believe Jesus is the true Son of God, Christ, who came to Earth to fulfill the Old Testament prophecy, to save sinners and the lost, and to defeat the evil one, the devil, Satan, or the fallen angel (alias Lucifer) and to cast away sin. God Himself came in human flesh as Jesus to provide enteral sal- vation to a world gone wrong, for no one can see Him, so He created Himself, as the son of man. God's form is in three parts: God the Father, God the Son, and God the Holy Ghost (Spirit). He works with us as in ways not known to man; some see Him as God, some see Him as Jesus, as for the third part, the Holy Spirit, He lives within all creation. Jesus came to this world to be born and live as a man in human form to see and suffer what man was going through.

God gave men free will and we (men) misused this wonderful gift of right or wrong. With weak minds man became cold and greedy. This was all Satan needed to know, the devil saw the weakness man had and this opened the door to men's damnation. Man could not resist the temptation of riches and power; men became blind with greed and the commandments of God had become forgotten. Remember God has gone through one evolution during the history of the earth, starting with the days of Noah, which is one of the most often criticized chapter man has tried to interpret.

God gave the first book to Moses called Genesis with the Ten Commandments and all the major themes and tablets of the history of life, containing the Old Testament and the New Testament. I must leave it there, for I am not a theologian or a person of expertise in theology, just what God has given me to share with you, that, that God has given me, and that I have listened to Him correctly and not confusing my readers.

We are one body in Christ. For every life has its purpose. Now where do we go from here? Hope, truth, and love. **But if we walk in the light he is the light** (1 John 4:7). "Beloved, let us love one another for love is of God: God is love. Praise God."

A prayer: Lord, I am but a simple trace of dust in your vast universe: and the window that you have given us to share with one another; we have so mis- understood and mistreated that, that you have given us, and in turn you have also given us your greatest gift, your beloved Son Jesus, and He too suffered for our transgressions, in hope that our forgiveness will be forgiven by you, our loving Father. Amen.

From everlasting to everlasting, thou are God:
Psalm 90:2

I am solely responsible for what I have written in this book; the Lord is my witness in this event that I have received, I have accepted what knowledge the Lord has given me; you must forgive me if I have confused any of you, but all that I have placed in this manuscript is with all my honesty and a revelation God has given me from the book I call, **"The King James Version Bible." Seek and you shall find; for everyone that asketh receiveth (Matthew 7:11).** Praise God.

Part 11

Where Are We?

Time seems to be going backward. Let us look back at the time of Noah; most of us are made to believe things were just as they were in the time of King David, approximately 1010 BC. The apparel of clothing worn was linen clothing wrapped around one's torso or a tunic. As for the days of Noah, we have no knowledge of what type of clothing they wore or what the world was like.

Was it as we see how the world is turning today? **For God destroyed all traces of the world and of man of that time.** Except for that, that Noah will bring with them into the ark? God told Noah he had to survive with what hand tools and what clothing they had at hand. Those were the only things Noah will bring with him on to the new world. With those hand tools, this must be the reason it took Noah so long to build the ark, as told by God. Knowing how advanced men were in Noah's time, this is a man who builds a vessel called the ark out of wood, a substance unlike metal—metal rusts and returns to dust— wood on the other hand, is unsinkable and it floats.

Tools of that time have never been found; were the people of that time so advanced beyond our compre- hension and imagination? Unknown to us what power or what tools they used, Noah on the other hand, had to use hand-me-down tools for the crafting of the ark that was made from a heavy grain timber called gopherwood.

All the many pictures that I have seen of the Ark seem to have been made from slabs cut from logs with modern tools as today. But Noah was told by God to use only the tools that he will bring with him into the new world, and therefore, it took him a good hundred years to build the ark; he had to split the logs with a line of chisels lined up along the top of the log and a large hammer to split the logs. The ark did not have precut boards or metal nails as seen in men's picture of the ark today. You must use your imagination. The way I picture the ark was a large raft; unlike like a boat, it did not have a keel nor rudder to guide the ark as a boat does; God was the pilot and in control.

Noah, knowing that this so-called gopherwood would not sink as metal does, knew the Lord was in control. I'm sure Noah was laughed at while making a large wooden raft with forgotten tools in a modern world of superior awareness, crafting, and design. Noah obeyed the Lord's word.   Gopherwood is an unidentified wood of that time; was it used in log form, or wood slabs split from the logs? If so, what type of tools did Noah use at that time? This is beyond our comprehension of a world not described therein (pre-flood). Noah was around 480 years old when this started, and about the age of 600, when he entered the ark. All the dates are hard to pinpoint. Gopherwood is a word unknown else- where other than the Bible. Had men become so pow- erful with the sinful using of the power given to them by a loving God?

The science fiction stories of men's imagination of today are coming true; men are going beyond the moon and playing with life form, creating cloned ani- mals and trying to create human form, and robots to replace man. Will God allow mankind to continue, or is Revelation beginning to prove the vials of God's wrath? **"And I heard a great voice out of the temple saying to the seven angels, 'Go your ways, and pour out the seven vials of wrath of God'" (Revelation 16:1).**

Is the Word of God being bedded, forsaken, and forgotten? This seems to be happening today.

People are being deceived by Satan, as Adam and Eve were in the Garden of Eden when Satan said, **"You shall not surely not die,"** making humans believe that they would become a God-like person praised by all like onto God Jehovah.

As for the broken spirit of God, we will never know, for He is a forgiving father. With God's gratefulness, He permitted man to live for many years at the time of Noah. Noah lived for 950 years; he became a father at the approximately 480 years of age, but all this is not really known. At the age of 500, Noah and his sons, Shem, Ham, and Japheth started to build the ark. Noah was 600 years old when he and his family entered the ark.

We have no idea how long a year was at time, other than a day was sun up to sun down. **"And God said let there be light: and there was light" (Genesis 1:3). "And God saw that the light was good: and God divided the light from the darkness" (Genesis 1:4). "And God called the light day, and the darkness he called night" (Genesis 1:5).** For all life of that time as we know it was destroyed, and so were all traces of life before Noah enter the ark, all removed with a world gone bad.

We read in our Bible and books of old about flying chariots found in book one of Ezekiel. The prophet describes flying chariots containing wheels within wheels and powered by angels. Bible historians are not sure how to explain what Ezekiel saw as flying machines. As for the time of Moses, men have found chariot wheels in the floor of the Red Sea where Moses was to have crossed the Red Sea. In the year of 2000 AD, evidence of chariots crossing the Red Sea and proving the history of Moses **(A must see on YouTube)** titled **"Chariot wheels in the Red Sea, part 2 & part 3, and Proof of the supernatural."** If this doesn't open your eyes, what can I say? Now back to the ancient history of men in Noah's time.

Unknown if Noah, ever told or wrote what it was like before he entered the ark. We have no deep evidence of that. The people had to have been intellectual; there is no way to explain any of this, for there is no trace or evidence that reveals the lifestyle pre-Noah's time, none that have ever been found prior to the flood; other than fossils of animals and organisms of a life gone by.

Again, there are no traces of tools of that time that have ever been found to my knowledge. As for traces of metallic objects buried in the ground for so many years will deteriorate; even the Egyptian pyramids hold no signs of how men moved those enormous and gigantic stone blocks of great precision; it cannot be explained how all this was done.

Unlike in the movies today, showing 1,000 men pulling an enormous stone blocks weighing well over two tons.

How then were the huge stones of master archi- tecture moved? The movement of those stones on the ground I can picture, but, the lifting of stones with such precise micro edges leaves me speechless and in wonderment. As for the carvings, there is no living proof how those works were done; and nobody today can explain how they were lifted! No! Neither manpower nor beast power are the answer; rope is out of the question. It is true the stones could have been moved on the ground by rolling logs. Those people had to have been beyond our imagination. The word levita- tion comes to mind; was there a magnetic force those people knew about now lost in time? I myself cannot believe a stonemason could have carved those Hugh stones with hand tools; this would have taken many days to create each statue, much less so many of them that look alike. What about laser technology like is being used today?

Unknown how long man lived before the flood in questionable; but the life span of a stonemason of that time after Adam and Eve sinned had to have been shortened, for man had a short life span after the flood.

The mystery of the history of the human race back then cannot be explained, and this would have taken many years to form such huge structures and pyra- mids found in the Sinai desert and throughout many parts of the world.

Today, with modern tools, it took Mount Rushmore fourteen years to form the four faces carved on rock; the carving began in 1927 and stopped in 1941, but those carvings were not lifted in place. I know I'm stepping out of my range, but, the prophecy I see in the Bible makes me wonder how intelligent and scientific those men were before the flood. This is becoming a true pic- ture of men of today; men who are looking beyond the stars for traces of lifeforms and God; all this has left men boggled trying to open the door to God's heaven. There is a new world promised to us by our Lord God Jehovah, He called it a new earth yet to come.

Now back to Noah's time. I wonder how Noah felt when God told him to bring with him into the ark a pair of all beasts, male and female, both clean and unclean?

As for the animals that entered the ark two by two are a mystery unknown. Other than what God told Noah, he did not question the Lord.

The ark was 450 x 75 x 45 feet. There were seven pairs of clean animals acceptable for sacrifice, and one pair of all other animals that were taken into the ark. Noah was first mentioned in the Bible (**Genesis 5:29**); he was at 480/500 years old when he received the order from God to build the ark. It is believed that it took Noah 120 years to build the ark. Noah was

600 years old by the time finished the ark and that would depend how much time had passed between Genesis 5:32 and the time that God commanded Noah to enter the ark.

As for the ark, why was the ark made from wood? Again, this is my interpretation. I believe everything was made very much like today; iron was used for large structures and all types of mobile crafts, so why was Noah told by God to build a wooden vessel that had not been used for many years in Noah's world? I will try to paint a picture with my interpretation.

God knew what was about to happen shortly, for life had become unstable, and overpowering in opposition of God's Word. Man became disobedient, as found in **Genesis 6:5. "And God saw the wickedness of man was great in the earth, and that every imagination of the thoughts of his heart was only evil continu- ally" (Genesis 6:6). "And it repented the Lord that he had made man on the earth, and it grieved him at his heart. And the Lord said, *I will destroy men whom I have created from the face of the earth*'" (Genesis 6:7).**

Here is my interoperation of that time. I believe the people of Noah's time were very intellectual, more than we can endeavor; though we have no known knowledge or history of that time. God has erased all traces of a world gone bad and nothing was left but what came in the ark. Let me start with my common knowl- edge as I see it in the making of the ark. So why did God tell Noah to use wood? We know iron (metal) will caustic and corrode in time and will deteriorate below the earth's surface, and wood will float and won't sink. So, understood by Noah, he started to gather a type of wood known as gopherwood, that God had commanded him to do so. Gopherwood is a term used once in the Bible, a wood substance which Noah's ark was to be built. The ark is to be plastered with pitch, a substance matter that has an oily base and it is water proofed after it dries. Let's move on.

Noah and his sons, Shem, Ham, and Japheth pre- pared and leveled a large lot in the back of their house and started to build a wooden craft unlike a typical vessel of that day. The making of ark of wood and pitch wasn't like a boat as we know today; it was a large wooden raft much longer than a football field; the ark was 450 feet long, 75 feet side to side, flat unlike a boat, and the height was 45 feet.

Where Noah and his family gathered the gopher- wood timber or how it was carried to side is not known. The way I see it, it took many years to finish the ark. The exact time it took Noah to build the ark is not spe- cifically mentioned in the Bible, other than it took Noah and his family at least 100 years to build. As Noah and his family were working on the ark, the passersby would laugh and hackle at the large square raft with only one window on the upper section above the ramp, built in the middle of a land with no sea or water ways for miles around. No one offered a helping hand to a crazy man using old and forgotten hand tools that had not been used for many, many years.

To the unbelievers, Noah and his family were just believers of a god that did not exist. It was a sorrowful and disgraceful world of non-believers lost in lust and sin beyond what we are seeing today. God knew Noah's family had to start in a new world with what few hand tools they could carry with them in the ark and what the earth would supply them with; this was well under- stood by Noah. The way I see it, is why it took so many years to finish the ark.

The exact time it took Noah to build the ark is not specifically mentioned in the Bible, other than 100 years of Noah's life before entering the ark. It was unusual for rain fall as we know it, and hard rain was not heard of, other than a heavy mist that started in the Garden of Eden **(Genesis 7:4).** Heavy rain became a new drama at that time.

A year had passed, and the time was at hand; about the seventh day after Noah had finished; changes had started to happen, the weather was becoming unpre- dictable. Noah gathered his family in prayer, for Lord God had told Noah that the time was at hand and it was time to open the gate on the ark, for this day the rain will start. The animals God had gathered were ready to enter the ark. The foolish hackers were laughing and pointing to see this event that was happening as God ordered Noah to lower the ramp.

Two by two, the animals started to enter the ark; first the seven pair of clean sacrificial animals fol- lowed by the unclean animals. Unknown what animals entered, I'll start with the cattle, and all the fore legged beasts such as horses, asses, camels, goats, and sheep, pigs and unfriendly animals, bears, deer, moose, and so forth; as for the dog family, came the wolf, coyotes, fox, jackals, and other breeds of dog-like animals; also, all birds of prey. Unlike today with so many different breeds that evolved from the day they enter the ark, the Bible only talks about the animals of that time.

So many changes have come with the evolution of time. As people emerged around the earth and they became a define race as they emerged from a cold tem- perature on to tropical climate turning their skin to pro- tect them from the weather changes. I believe all beasts are related to one another as humans are. After animals interbreeding with one other, they became a new cre- ation of the many different breeds of animals of today.

What about the large beasts, such the dinosaurs? I believe the flood took care of that. For every breed in life there is a reason, from man to beast, clean and unclean, from the smallest germ to the largest form of beast, also trees, shrubs, and vegetation. Let us go on. **"And it came to pass after seven days' that the waters of the flood were upon the earth" (Genesis 7:10). "In the six hundredth year of Noah's life, in the second month, the seventeenth day of the month, the same day of the flood were all the foun- tains of the great deep broken up, and the win- dows of heaven were opened" (Genesis 7:11). "And the rain was upon the earth forty days, and forty nights" (Genesis 12).**

As the rain became heavier and the waves pounded on the ark's sides, people gasped for air and life all around the ark, but it was of no use, for God had done what He had promised Noah was to happen.

We are the creation of the Lord God; with a process yet to come.

"He that has an ear, let him hear what the spirit said unto the churches: to him who overcome will

I give to eat of the tree of life, which is in the mist, of the Paradise of God" (Revelation 2:7).

These visions are given to me by God, I will try to interpret and make them simple to understand. It is not what happened before Noah entered the ark that worries me. It's what is happening today and the future of man to come. Is it a repeat? **"As for as the days of Noah were, so will the coming of the Lord be." (Matthew 24:37).**

In the days of Noah, disobedience overcame men, man went against God's will; the earth was corrupt before God. **"And the earth was filled with violence, and God saw that the wickedness of man was great in the earth, and the Lord repented that he had made man on the earth, and it grieved him at his heart" (Genesis 6:5).**

Book 2

Part 12

Noah Before the Flood

When I first started this book the title I had picked was **"Noah Before the Flood"**, but as I went on, it turned out to be my vision of the King James Bible. As I continued I realized what I was writing was something so different, and that some- thing has happened to me, I realized my interpretation of that time was something from the Lord, something He had placed in my mind. Not being very knowledge- able with the Bible, I knew enough to understand the Word and what the Lord was laying in my mind, so I continued. Now going on with what I intended to do, that is, **"The story of Noah before the flood."**

What I'm writing about in this story is not really explained in the Bible. This is my interpretation of a prophecy as I see it. Jesus gave us a warning. Turn to **Matthew 24:37.** The Lord said, ***"But, as the days of Noah were, so shall also the coming of the son of man be."*** This passage I keep repeating in my mind, which makes me believe that the ways things are going today is a repeat of what had happened after Adam and on to the time of Noah, for there are no known evidence as to what the world was truly like at that time, for God removed all traces of all living flesh and all living substances He had made and removed them from the face of the earth; for God saw that the wickedness of man was great and it repented the Lord that He had made man and other living creatures on the earth **(Genesis 6:5).** These are the things that are told to us in the book of Genesis expressing what the world had gone through, and it seems to be repeating the same pattern today.

Adam had fathered many children and the world began to increase that by the time Noah had come to existence some 216 years after the death of Adam, the population had to have increased heavily.

There were ten generations between Adam and Noah. Now let's put a little science fiction to explain how I vision the time before Noah and how I interpret my vision making it come to life. Adam reached the age of 937 years and had many sons and daughters that were born to him and Eve. These children increased in the same manner as their descendants. The people of that era lived for eight or nine hundred years as the population greatly increased. The record of time men- tions only the fact that people had increased in wick- edness and immoral ways that God so greatly repented that He had made them, and He brought upon the world the great flood.

God decided, and in conclusion, that He will destroy every living creature except those who were preserved in the ark which Noah prepared under the Lord's direc- tion. Of all the descendants of the Sethite who ignored the morals of God, only Noah and his family were saved. Noah and his three sons, Shem, Ham, and Japheth, were 120 years in the completing of the gigantic ark to fulfill what God had command Noah to do. It is dif- ficult to write about the times of a world we have no knowledge of, but the Lord gives us a way to express the things we acknowledge from His word.

What you see is different from what I envision. My vision of the time before Noah is a representation of what I interpret as to what the times were like, and of that, that we have no knowledge. Now the way I inter- pret the story of Noah and envision what the Lord has given me as I write.

Let's imagine that the time of Noah's was like the science-fiction stories shown today on TV and in the movies of today; no one really knows what it was like before Noah entered the ark, for God removed all the things that happened before the flood. Looking at the way things are going today, it looks like a repeat.

For Jesus told us about the event that is to come. **"The coming of the Son of Man."** This only tells me that men of that time were advanced in technology.

I feel we are heading in that direction. Let's imagine that life in Noah's world was like the life in the Buck Rodgers movies, or the cartoon movie of the Jetsons, with intelligence of the future of man in space. I will leave it there and start my story about the way I see the life of Noah's world before the flood.

Part 13

A Man Called Noah

It's unknown where Noah was born, so I will call it the city of U-Nia. (You Knee Uh). It does not really exist! U-Nia was the largest city of that time; it had the best university known to man. U-Nia also had the best knowledgeable men in science technology, they were so advanced in the technology of space and in oceanography, and man could travel to and from one place to another with trance-air vehicles.

As for Noah and his family, they lived in the low- land about seven miles from the city of U-Nia; it was farm land passed on to Noah by his father.

The world was in turmoil with so many unfaithful adulterers, cheaters, and unbelievers of the deity of God. Noah did not approve of the changes of that time; there was no unity amongst any of them to be shared. It was dreadful to mention the very Word of God, for the world had gone astray and sinful. They would trade their bodies for any favor they needed. Adultery was the thing for pleasures between man with man or woman by woman or multi-gathering, in a world of wow. The commandments of God were placed aside and never mentioned in those times. Even the so-called righteous had steered away.

Noah and his family had settled in the valley away from the city limits I call U-Nia. His father was named Lemech, one of the only believers left from Adam's past, now known as the Canaanites who were Idlers. As for Noah, he lived a life of righteousness and raised his family the best he could, for he knew God was the way and the truth.

Let's pretend that the times were like in science-fic- tion stories as told today, for no one really knows what it was like back then, for God removed all things that happened before the flood. Looking at the way things are going today, it looks like a repeat; for Jesus told us about the event that is to come. I repeat: **"But as the days of Noah were, so shell the coming of the Son of Man be." (Matthew 25:37).** Men were advanced in technology, and space travel. I feel we are heading in that direction. The people of Noah's time had a much higher intelligence than we do today and that shows me that we are heading in the same direction. Let us imagine that life was like in the time of the Buck Rodgers movie, or the cartoon of the Jetsons animated life in the future of space.

Early one morning, Noah had to travel to the city of U-Nia to pay his surcharges. Being a poor farmer, he had no transportation or trans-air vehicles as the people of that time had, with him it was walking to and from as he did that day.

He neared the garden plaza; a large rock monument was the only entrance to that part of the city. As he was entering, he encountered three men involved in an unnatural behavior at the side of the wall, unlike dogs; Noah walk on.

As Noah passed through the entrance in this city of wow, he encountered two other men; one of the men reached out and grabbed his arm and said to him, "Come and enjoy our party." They were naked, and this took Noah by surprise. Noah was aware of these type of things that were going on, but he never thought that he would ever encounter this type of behavior that was just happening to him. Not knowing what to do, his thoughts were to pray to God for an answer, for he was a believer of the Lord God and to him this was an abomination against the Lord's word.   About that time the men grabbed him and were forcefully dancing as they tidily held on to him. Noah had to think of something, for he knew he had to be careful not to agi- tate or ruffle them as he was forced to dance along.

Thinking quickly, he said, "My friends, if you can be patience, let me go pay my surcharges to the governor and I will be more than glad to come back and enjoy and, relax with you."

The two looked at each other released his arms and danced around him. One replied; "Oh dear one, we will be waiting, don't take too long."

What a relief came upon Noah. With his heart pounding profusely, he went on. The two men waved as Noah rushed on his way, thanking the Lord. With hope, he knew he had to find a new passage home; what a story he had to tell his wife.

After he had finished his business with his taxes, he walked out the door thinking of a different way to go, for he did not want to encounter with that sinful group he just bumped into at the garden gate.

Noah had walked a few squares not familiar to him, hoping to go around the rock entrance and not to be seen by the party group he had encountered earlier. But, this was the only way out, the rock entrance. He stopped where he could see the group had gotten larger and were taking their clothes off. He stopped and won- dered how to pass them without being noticed. Luck was with him, for it happened that one of the men in the bunch had a day of celebration.

They removed his clothing and picked him up and placed up on one of the park table, all eyes were on him. Noah was in heavy thought, thinking of how to bypass them without being noticed, when a thought came to him; that is to remove his upper garment exposing his upper body pretending he was one of them by removing his garments as many were doing. Quietly, he passed the crowd without being noticed. He praised God as he placed his clothing back on and continued his way home.

When he arrived home, Hancel, his wife was waiting for him. She was so excited she ran up to him. They embraced what a welcome this was to Noah after what he had gone through that morning. She started to talk, but Noah was so excited about what he had gone through and wanted to tell her, so, he went on with his story. Hancel could not be still and this stopped Noah, wondering why she was so excited.

He looked at her and said, "Why are you so excited? Is something wrong?"

"Well if you must know, you better take a seat and I'll tell you."

Noah looked at her in wonderment. She smiled and softly said, "I – I am with child."

"You are what?" Noah loudly replied. He picked her up and started dancing around and around with her in his arms; how wonderful the day had become with two exciting adventures.

It is written that it had taken Noah some 500 years before he started to have a family. He was so thankful. A few years had gone by, and Noah had three sons. He named them Shem, then Ham and Japheth.

One day, Noah and his sons were working the in the field planting wheat and corn, and they were running out of seeds, so Noah took the ass and went to get some seed from the back of the house. He felt something strange was happening, as if someone was looking at him. He dropped to his knees and leaned against the sack of seeds, giving thanks to God.

Noah was a poor farmer who had no modern equip- ment; everything he had was hand-me-downs that came from his family, but he was thankful he had a loving wife, three great sons, and a small parcel of land.

Noah had a heart of gold, not one selfish bone, and much consideration for others. The citizens of the city of U-Nia would look down on Noah as an ignorant person who believed in a God that did not exist. Noah was an outcast from society of non-believers who were lost in a life of sin. Noah went on with his life.

As time went by, Noah's sons had taken themselves wives. Life became much easier for Hancel; she taught them how to make cheese, bake bread, and how to clean foul, lamb, and so forth. Life was hard for them but, love made their life joyful. The people on Earth were wicked, and men begun to multiply in all parts of the world, beyond the city of U-Nia.

God saw the wickedness of men was great in the earth, and that every imag- ination of the thoughts of his heart was only evil continually. And it repented the Lord that he had made men on the earth and it grieved him at his heart. *And the Lord said, "I will destroy man whom I have created from the face of the earth; both man and beast, and*

the creeping thing, and the fowls of the air; for it repenteth me that I have made them." (Genesis 6:5-7)

The morning of the great event had arrived. Noah was in the stable working on his plow when a voice echoed around him saying, *"Noah."* He turned and saw no one; he thought it was one of his sons. He went back to his work and once again, he was summoned. This time, the voice echoed out strongly, *"Noah."* Noah realized it was the Lord who had summoned him. "Here am I, Lord," he bowed, for the presence of the Lord was very powerful.

And God said to Noah,

> *"The end of all flesh is come before me; for the earth is filled with vio- lence through them; and behold I will destroy them with the earth"* (Genesis 6:13, / 6:19).

This left Noah frightened as to why the Lord told him this; he did not question the Lord's word and he humbled himself onto God, as He continued:

> *"Make thee an ark of gopherwood; rooms shall thou make in the ark and shall pitch it within and without with pitch, make it of; the length of the ark shall be three hundred cubits, the breadth of it fifty cubits, and the height of it thirty cubits. A window shalt thou make to the ark, and in a cubit shalt finish it above; and the door of the ark thou set in the side thereof; with lower; second and third stories shalt thou make it. And behold I even I, do bring a flood of waters upon the earth, to destroy all flash, wherein is the breath of life, from under heaven; and every-thing that is in the earth shall die. But with the, I establish my covenant; and thou shall come into the ark, thou, and thy sons, and thy wife*

and thy sons' wives with thee. And of every living thing of all flesh, two of every sort shalt thou bring into the ark".

Noah had no idea where to start; he knelt to give thanks unto the Lord. He was frightened and somewhat excited and wanted to tell the family, but he thought it over to wait until suppertime when all the family would be together.

Later that evening, one by one, all came to the table, and they sat and held hands and Shem gave grace. Noah waited until everyone had finished eating, for what he was to present to them would startle them.

Hancel noticed Noah was quiet, and he had not touched his food, but she didn't say anything at that time. A little time passed, and she had to say some- thing, "Dear, is something wrong? You haven't touched your food."

He sighed and took a deep breath. Ham said, "What happened? Papa! Did the ass kick you and you had to plow the field by hand?" They all laughed, all but Noah.

He thumped on the table with his cup and this brought their attention; everyone stopped talking. "My loved ones," he paused, took a deep breath, and said, "I have something important to tell all of you."

They all thought something might have happened to him. He continued. "Today–when I was in the barn and—and the Lord God spoke to me." They all looked at him; he had a serious look about him, wondering why he was saying this. He said, "No, no the Lord God spoke to me. What I'm going to tell you may scare you." They all had his attention, as he spoke again. "The Lord God said on to me that the end of time is at hand." A silence came about them; their hearts started pounding with fear. Noah was also afraid of the unknown. He continued explaining, "The Lord told me that the

end of all flesh is come for the earth is filled with vio- lence throughout; and that everything that has life on Earth shall die, then, the Lord also said, 'But I have established my covenant with you, for I have found favor within you; you will build an ark of gopherwood;' rooms thou shall make in the ark and shall pitch it within and without with pitch, He also told me what animals I must take with me, and that you my family will be spared and by my side."

Nothing was being said, as fear multiplied among them all. They tried to comfort each other as they held hands. Noah continued, "God told me not to be afraid for the comforter (the Holy Spirit) shall be with us in the ark."

This opened the family with questions, all babbling at the same time. Noah once again pounded his cup on the table. And silence came once again as he said, "I will point who is to speak, I know how you must feel; I will start with the eldest, that would be you, Shem."

It took Shem a few moments before he spoke, "Papa are you sure – sure, that it was the Lord that spoke to you? You have been working very hard of late and you may have dozed off."

Noah would not let Shem finish; he said, "Son, have I ever misled any of you, what makes you doubt my word." "Father, you have scared us by saying what you claim was the Lord talking to you." Shem stood up shaking his head and walked out the door. He returned a few moments later and sat quiet. Noah looked at him and said, "My son, I will start to build the ark as told to me by God, and I will need you all of you to help me." No one said a word, but the silence was broken by Japheth saying, "Papa, how do you expect to build this so-called ark? We are farmers and where do you expect to get all this gopherwood that it will take to make this so-called ark?"

Shem stood up said, "All this sounds so, so igno- rant; I will have nothing to do with it." He took his wife and went into the other room.

Noah said nothing, and the rest of the family stood quiet and frightened. He said, "I will do as my Lord commends me, even if none of you will help."

With eyes full of tears, Noah went into his room and dropped to his knees to pray, when the voice spoke to him. ***"Noah, thy will be done you will have many setbacks, but you will prevail for the Lord God has spoken and will make those with you prevail also; so be it."***

At that moment Hancel walked in and said, "Who were you talking to? I heard voices?"

Noah looked up at her and said, "It was the angel of God who came to confirm what God has told to me to do, and I will build the ark."

Hancel agreed with Noah and said, "I will be by your side, for we are one." Noah was pleased to know his wife so believed on him and she was on his side.

A few days had passed Noah had taken time to make plans for the ark and was ready to share with his family, so he decided to summon all of them and come to see what the Lord had shared with him, but, he had to wait till his boys finished their chores.

He placed the tablet he had made on the large table under the shade of one of the trees. It was incredible what seemed impossible for a simple man like Noah, a common farmer who had no knowledge in architec- tural planning coming up with the plans for the ark.

It was a warm day and his sons came in a little bit earlier for the sun was a bit uncomfortable that day. After they cleaned themselves, it was time to relax. They went to the back where their father was waiting for them. Hancel and the girls had made refreshments for them all. Noah was happy that they were all there. He summoned them together to share his works the Lord had presented to him. Noah walked them over to where the large table was. Their eyes opened wide to see what was placed on that table and wondering where he had, had the prints made.

The family just stood looking at each other. Shem had to ask where he had the prints made. "Well son," replied Noah, "this is what the Lord has given me, I have no other answer." Noah noticed the doubtfulness on their faces; he looked at them and said, "I have made all you see on this table, this is what will help us step by step as soon as we start making the ark."

Ham said, "Papa, you did this?"

Noah smiled, and replied, "Yes son, with the help of the Lord, all things are possible."

Shem took seconds thought about what his father had implied when he told them that the Lord God had spoken to him, he had no more doubt.

"We will start as soon as possible," replied Noah. Shem spoke up. "Father, how long will all this take? We have the fields to tend; again, Papa, I say, how long will it take to make this huge unbelievable thing call the ark, and where do we get this so-called gopherwood? We don't have that kind of wood around here, Papa."

Noah replied, "Son, it will take as long as it takes; the Lord gave me no time limit he just told me to start as soon as posable, his work will be done; as for you women, you will have to carry on with the field work and you will have learn to make pitch as God requires me to seal the ark with. I know the Lord will give you strength to carry on."

The boys talked it over and asked Noah as to where they are to get the gopherwood. Noah replied to them, "I took a walk to the foothills to where the forest starts, and the angel of God appeared to me, and he walked me to a dense part of the forest and pointed to the many trees God had chosen. It will take much work, but it will be done."

Japheth who was the one who took care of the two mules and the ass spoke up. "Papa, we only have the two mules and the ass and a small wagon, this will take us forever."

"Son, this I will leave it up to the Lord, now let us pray. Dear Lord God, we shall get started and with thy will, we are ready to prepare the way you have appointed me to do, that is to build an ark as you have assigned me. God, thy will be done, Amen."

Part 14

A Time to Start–A Time to Rip.

There is no set time when all this had happened except that Noah was around 500 years of age when Noah begat Shem, Ham, Japheth. The inspired record indicates Noah's sons were already grown and married when God commanded Noah to build the Ark. Unknown to them that the building of the Ark required a long time and involved a great deal of arduous hard labor.　　Noah and his sons had leveled a parcel part of the land facing the east side of the house where the well was, so when water was needed, they didn't have to depend on someone having to carry water to the site. It took them more than three months to level the side. The corral for the animals was moved elsewhere.

Now it was time to start the voyage to gather the gopherwood that God has commended Noah to build the ark with. First thing Noah had to do was to build a sled that the mules could pull when loaded with gopherwood, a wood that was heavier than other type of trees; the timber was strong and resistant to water.

As his boys leveled the lot where the ark was to be built, Noah was hard at work with the sled he had designed. The hardest part to make were the iron rails that will replace the wheels. The sled was made into two sections; the short section was placed in front and would turn the sled when needed with a unique pulling lever. Next was the braking unit; this was a tricky and unusual setup placed in the back section of the sled where the breaking unit was placed.

Noah made two small plow blades that would dig into the ground when the lever was applied; they were placed under the sled. It took Noah about six months to finish his work.

It was the third day of the fifth month into the begin- ning of second year; they were ready to go seek for the gopherwood that the angel had shown Noah a few months back. The tools that were used at that time is unknown, for Noah had no modern tools or levitation magnetic equipment; everything they used was man- ually handled.

When they arrived at the forest where the angel had taken Noah, to their surprise many of the trees were marked and they all seemed to be of the same radius. Was this the works of the Lord? Not one of them had doubts. By day's end, the first load was ready to haul; the mules were hitched to the sled, and it was time to start moving. To their surprise, the poor mules could not pull the load. The load was way too heavy; this wood was known for its density and hardness. The load was reduced; now, the mules could pull the sled. They knew that it was going to take longer due to the weight of the lumber.

On the way home, Noah and his boys noticed that the city of U-Nia was expanding and spreading closer to their property; this was new to them, for they had not paid any attention to what was going on at the front of their property for more than couple of years due to the work on the ark. The main road was being worked on near his front property, and this worried Noah. That night, Noah had a talk with his family that he was going to go have a talk with the governor, and to also tell them what the Lord has revealed to him. He knew this would be difficult knowing they were non-believers.

A few days had passed, and the pile of gopherwood was sky high and the road workers were taking notice. They gathered around, wondering what Noah was up to. This was brought up to the city governor. Noah did not have to go downtown to have a talk with him. The governor and many delegates came by early next day.

That morning Noah and the family were alarmed when Ham walked in very excited, for he saw a multi- tude of people had gathered at the new road that had been built recently. The roadway was filled with many people and crafts of all different types not known to

Noah. He prepared himself and the boys to go talk to them. Noah was in heavy prayer within, not knowing how he was to approach this crowd. The governor came up to Noah. Noah greeted them; the governor replied by saying, "What are all these piles of logs you have gathered for?"

Noah posed momentarily then said, "I have been told by God All Mi—!"

He didn't have a chance to finish. The crowd had become rowdy and noisy, and the governor had to intervene, for he wanted to hear what this foolishly godly man had to say, and he wanted them all to hear also. He ordered a hover platform to lift Noah where he could be seen by all.

Noah did not have any fear, for he knew he was doing the Lord's work. He was ordered to step on the platform that levitated him to a set height. Noah, with a loud voice, started his word of warning to all. **"The Lord God has spoken to me."**

This started the crowd to go out of control with booing and laughter, for they were all non-believers. Once again, the governor had to tame the unruly crowd; this time he had to summons the guards to take con- trol. After things settled down, Noah had the platform once again.

"I was told by God Jehovah to build an Ark, for the end of time is at hand. He also told me that a rain will come, and a flood will overtake the world and all living things will be destroyed and nothing with life shall be spared. God also told me to build an ark, and I will do that, and you should also do the same. I cannot be more specific than this, for the world is corrupted with sin, violence, and adultery; so, says the Lord. I know that I am, but a simple man given this great command- ment by the Almighty God Jehovah, please take this to be true."

The governor turned to the crowd, and everyone busted out laughing. He turned back and said to Noah, "So you are going to build a boat – I, I mean, an ark, as you call it? Well I am sorry to be the one to tell you this, but you will have to put wheels on that ark, for there is no sea around these parts for miles, and I'm sure you will have a hard time pulling it with two mules, and one ass."

The crowd with much laughter was amused and started to leave. Noah stepped down from the hov- er-unit. The governor and his staff walked away with much laughter. Once again, Noah hollered loudly, "You must listen to my warning, my warning." It was of no use. His sons summoned their father to come on home, for it was of no use talking to heathens. Noah wondered if he had let God down, then he realized what God had told him was true.

The family gathered at back of the house. Noah had a talk with them. "We must carry on with the Lord's work, no matter what." All agreed.

Now the time had come for Noah to start the ark layout. They were a few things he needed that he did he not have yet; one was small branches to make dowel pegs, for no iron is to be used on the ark. This was not questioned, only that wood would swell when wet and tightened. Another thing was animal skin to make straps to tie the timber together. Noah took his son Ham with him to gather gopherwood branches to make the pegs. They took the two mules and the sled and a few tools to cut the limbs. They were gone for about four hours. On their return home, Noah took Ham to the shed at the back of the house to teach him how to make the pegs of different sizes. Ham was the artistic one in the family, and the pegs had to be certain size and placed in the correct sized holes and pounded in place.

That evening, Noah studied the prints under can- dlelight, for they did not have modern lighting; it was too costly. Awakened by morning light, Noah was ready to start the main keel. This is the longest part of the ark. The keel is the main home brace to the ark. All branches are attached to keel; this is the backbone and the largest part that attaches all the side ribs on to it.

It took them more than four years to put the keel together at the length of 450 feet. (*One must remember Noah had primitive tools, for the Lord was preparing Noah with what he is to survive with, and to exist in the new world set before him.*) No one in U-Nia would give Noah a helping hand, for he was a freak who believed in an imaginary, make-believe God who supposedly told him to build the ark in a place with no waterways for miles around.

The average logs were cut to twenty-eight feet in length, and the short eight-foot logs were placed and centered on the end of the twenty-eight-foot log. All logs were joined together with dowel pins dipped patch, and leather straps throughout the keel. (the main lower timber section).

Now came the tricky part: how to join the bottom log attachment to the keel. Two notches were made, one to the top of the main keel and the other to the side rib. The bottom floor took more than seven years to put together; the walls for the rooms was the easiest; those took about five years six months, maybe longer. Next was the second floor that took another long extenua- tion of time. The length of time was not a factor to them.

Now came the most crucial part of the engineering; this was the side of the ark where the ramp to the entrance was to be placed. It took Noah a long, long time and much studying as how to make the parts to where they would fit and work appropriate, and cor- rectly; everything had to be precise with accuracy. He had to make the gears that have never been made from wood; this included trust rods and pullies, all had to be heavy-duty. The women made the rope out of hide, and this took many days of braiding. The braided ropes were tested by lifting four twenty-eight-foot lodges on a pulley that hung over a heavy branch on one of the trees; none of the ropes failed.

Meanwhile the boys made the upper section with the only window ordered by God. Noah had a large area laid out to lay the parts of the ramp, making sure the parts were in order as he made them. This project took a long time to complete.

Many years had passed, and the ark was almost finished. The whole ark was pitched in and out as told to Noah by God. Pitch was made by the women; it took much time to cook the black substance for the water- proofing that was carried from the oil pit some distends from the house.

Not one day want by that the hecklers would walk by and loudly utter dirty remarks and blaspheme to them and God. Noah tried to get them to repent by warning them about the rain and the flood yet to come. Rain was not a factor back then; the moisture mostly came up from the ground that kept the earth green with foliage.

As Noah and his sons worked the final touches of the ark, Noah told his family that he had to have a little rest and give thanks to the Lord God Jehovah, and that he was taking a walk up the hill in the back and have a look at what they had accomplished. No one said a word as he took off toward the hillside. He sat under the shade of a bush and rested for a short while; as he looked at the ark, he could not believe what a huge sight he was looking at. It is said that it took Noah 120 years to finish the Ark. He kneeled to give thanks to the Lord, and God spoke to Noah. ***"Son of man."***

"Here am I, my Lord," replied Noah.

> *"You have done my will, you have lis- tened to my command now you have one more command".*
> The Lord God continued.

> *"Thou shall come into the ark, thou and thy sons, and thy wife, and thy sons' wives, with thee. And of every living thing of all flash, two of every sort shalt thou bring into the ark, keep them alive with thee, they shall be male and female. Of fowls after their kind, and of cattle after their kind, of every creeping thing of the earth after his kind, two of every sort, shall come unto thee, keep them alive. And take thou unto thee of all food that is eaten, and thou shall gather it to thee; and it shall be food for thee, and for them. Of every clean beast thou shall take to thee by sevens, the male and his female: and of the beasts that are not clean by two, the male and his female. Of fowls also of the air by sevens, the male and the female; to keep seed alive upon the face of all the earth for yet seven days I will cause it to rain upon the earth forty days and forty nights; and*

**every living substance that I have made will I destroy
from the face of the earth." (Genesis 6:18 /7:1-4)**

Noah listened and obeyed the Lord's command. He hurried down the hill and ran into the house with the news. Everyone gathered around him. Noah, breathing heavily, said, "The Lord has spoken to me; He told me that the rains will start in seven days, for forty days and forty nights, and said He will supply me with ani- mals and fowls of the air that will come with us into the ark; the Lord said to me we must gather domestic animals which we will use for food, fowl and lamb; this, Lord told me to do so, along with a large supply of grain and other food. The Lord told me not to worry about water; He will supply us with it."

At day's end, all was done as told to Noah by God. After supper, Noah and family took time to rest. Noah gathered them to give grace on to the Lord. He said, "Now we must wait for His command." It was time to bed down for the night.

The next morning, everyone was eating breakfast except for Ham; he went to milk the goats. It wasn't long before he came back in excited. Everyone stopped and looked up at him. Excitedly, he said, **"Papa! Papa!** The animals – the animals are all around, so many different — ah! Well. you have to come and see for yourself."

Everyone hurried outside. What a surprise of expression came on their faces to see so many kinds of animals of all types; many of those animals were vicious and one would not dare come near them, for they were fearful and dangerous. Noah decided to walk up to see if it was safe. He came near a lion and lioness; to his surprise he felt the gentleness and walked up to him. The lion rubbed against him and Noah rubbed the lion's head. He turned, and the family started to advance slowly toward him. All the animals were so gentle, so went the day.

In the city of U-Nia, the news had arrived at the gov- ernor's presence, and he said, "What now? What has that holy man come up with this time?"

"Sir, you won't believe what he has done; he has gathered so many different types of wild and vicious animals around his home; it's unbelievable, sir."

The governor replied, "These I have to see for myself;
now, call for my hovering craft."

When it arrived, the governor hovered in his craft around the site. He had a bit of trouble getting there because of the huge crowd. He wondered how did all this array of unusual animals had gotten there? The governor said, "I will go and ask this wired holy-man how all this came about; now open the gate."

One of his security guards said to him, "Sir, the gate will not open."

"What! It's just a common gate, what do you mean you can't open it?" he climbed off his hover-craft, walked to the gate, and tried to open it; the gate was unlocked, but it would not open. As they struggled with the gate, Noah arrived, ready to talk with them.

Noah said, "I have tried to warn you what is to come shortly, but you have negated my warning. You must repent from your wicked ways, for the wrath of God Almighty is at hand; you only have a short time." "You foolish man," replied the governor. "Why don't you go back to your rat hole? I'll have my guards come and remove you and all your pets, am I making myself clear?" Noah replied, "I have warned you and you do not want to take heed to my warning, may the Lord God

Jehovah, have mercy on all of you."

Noah was on his way back to the house, when the voice of the Lord spoke, ***"Noah! Hear me, the time is at hand, go open the gate to the ark, gather your family and enter the ark, the animals I God, have gathered are ready to enter therein."***

"It will be done, my Lord."

The crowd, laughing loud, thought Noah was talking to himself. Noah assembled his family in prayer for the time was at hand; it was time to open the gate on the ark. Noah and Sham walked to the side of the ramp, one on one side and the other on the other side. As they pulled on the ropes that released the ramp-gate, the gate slowly started to open; the foolish hackers all were pointing and laughing to see this event taking place in front their eyes. Noah and his family entered first, fol- lowed by the animals. What a sight to see the animals entering the ark two by two. First, the seven pair of clean sacrificial animals followed by unclean animals.

After the gate to the Ark slammed shut, everyone was laughing, singing, dancing, and embracing each other. Many held hands dancing around the ark **when** a lightning so forceful slammed across the entire sky. At that moment, all the satellites and the communi- cation responders that filled the skies above dropped back to Earth and left them without contact. The dark clouds started to gather rapidly as the rain started to fall so forcefully and violently, everyone started run-ning, not knowing which way to go.

Many ran up to the ark, yelling and begging for forgiveness and to open the ramp, but to no avail. As the waters rose upon the sides of the ark, the people screamed in panic, but not one called on the name of the Lord.

"This was the six hundredth year of Noah's life. The second month, the seventeenth day of the month, were, when the fountains of the great deep broken up and the windows of heaven were opened" (Genesis 7:11). It was a sad day for God, for His tears were falling upon the earth. It became a fearful day, and an unbelievable moment of fear for the unbeliever.   Many of the unbelievers gathered around the ark, yelling and shouting and unable to swim in any direction; it was of no use, for the Lord had done what He had promised Noah. **(This was the year of the flood, 1665 AM, Anno Mundi.) The rain was upon the earth forty days, and forty nights (Genesis 7:12).** As the rain became heavier and the waves pounded on the sides of the ark, a thought came to mind: was there trauma to all within? The way I see it, is the way the ark had been built, it's possible that it was not noticeable to those inside, for the Lord had placed his aura around the ark.

Another thought came to me! What about the lighting in the ark? What, other than candles, was used? This is not known, for the Ark had no windows, except the one on the upper section.   What the about the ani- mals? Did God put all the animals to sleep? Except for the animals on the upper level where the only window was placed, and Noah had control therein? (Just a thought in my mind.)

As the waters rose, covering the hills and mountain- tops so high, and hundreds of hundreds of humans and wildlife were buried under the waters that covered the earth, it was rather hard for Noah and his family, but they endured by keeping busy taking care of the animals. The women would make candles and clothing, just waiting for that day of triumph that the Lord had promised them.

For 150 days, the waters covered the earth. God made a wind to pass over the earth and the waters assuaged. After the rain had ceased, the wind began to blow, and calm came upon the earth and gradually the floodwaters receded.

Forty days had passed; now it was time for Noah to open the window, what glory came upon them when the soft wind entered the ark. They started singing praises to the Lord. The fresh air also reached the animals. This was an exciting moment for them all, man and beast alike, for the judgment of God was accom- plished **(Genesis 8:7-8).**

Now it was time for Noah to send forth a raven, knowing the raven was capable to fly a long distance without stopping. With no results, seven days later, a dove was released, but did not find a place to rest, so the dove returned to the ark.

Another seven days had passed, and Noah sent the dove on another flight, and this time the dove returned with an olive leaf that indicated dry land was upon the earth once more. Noah waited another seven days and once again sent the dove for the third time, and this time, the dove did not return.

The following day, mid-day, the ark bottomed out, for the water had receded and Noah discovered the land around was dry.

The ark in the seventh month on the seventeenth day of the month rested upon the mountain side of Ar'-a-rat. God spoke on to Noah that it was time for him and his family to leave the ark and to release the animals.

The animals were released; many gathered at a stream nearby to drink the water coming down from the hill. As to what happened to the animals? God, all-powerful, moved the animals thousands of miles all around the earth by His command. Noah and his family gathered many things that were needed out of the ark, to take with them on to the new world they were promised to them by a loving God.

Part 15

A Welcome to the New World

The time had come; it was time to leave the ark. Noah and his family stepped out of the ark; the first thing Noah had in mind was to build a stone altar and render a blood offering to thank God. The women had built a fire and started to cook for the first time outdoors, and soon they all gathered and gave grace to God. After a short rest, it was time to prepare and time to abandon the ark. In the ark, Noah had brought three wagons with them; the wagons were being loaded by all of them except for Japheth, who was taking care of the domestic animals. He had to build two wooden cages: one for the chickens and another for the small animals. By day's end, all their chores were finished and placed in the wagons. Noah gathered the family together to give thanks to Lord once again.

Noah said, "Please, let's hold hands." He started his prayer, "Our Father, hail be thy name; you havebrought us to this new world unfamiliar to us; we have no idea which way we must go, but I know you will show us the way, for thy will be done; we are so grateful Father, we will go on; from everlasting to everlasting thou are God."

They had settled down to rest when Shem said, "Father, with your permission, why don't you and I go to the top of that ridge up yonder? From there we can see the valley below, and maybe we can plan a way to continue with our journey."

"Very well said, Shem," replied Noah. "Let us go; we still have daylight for some three hours."

When they reached the hilltop, their eyes could not believe the view that was before them. In the far, far distance, they could see a valley with two separate rivers, later known as the Tigris and the Euphrates, but due to the distance this was far out of their minds.

Noah looked up at Shem and said, "Which way shall we go, son?"

They looked at each other when a mist fell upon them and the voice of the Lord spoke and said, ***"My children, you will follow my bow, I have set before you, my spirit will be with you, go in peace."***

They saw the rainbow, in the distance above the two rivers, and they did not question the distance after what the Lord had told them, and with much glory they hurried to where the family was waiting.

They were all thankful, and they shared what they had seen and received from the Lord God that day. It was time for them to settle down for the night.

Noah lay near his wife, both looking at the sky. They had never seen the sky this beautiful; the stars were as brilliant as diamonds and breathtaking, not like in U-Nia where the atmosphere was hazy all the time. Noah reached over and took hold of Hencel's hand and said, "God has given us a new life and glory and placed us here in a paradise never seen by man, we must humble ourselves and be thankful, for what was done in the past cannot be undone; we are here in the new world as God promised, we must carry on."

Hancel firmly squeezed Noah's hand and said, "We shall carry on, my husband." And quietly they fell asleep.

The next morning the rooster crowed for the first time; the break of day was so beautiful with the sun peeping from the east. One by one, they went to the drain hole to relieve themselves. Noah had a fire going with a tub of water warming up for them to clean them- selves. The women were making breakfast, and his boys were getting things ready to go just as soon as breakfast was over.

It was the second day; they did not have a time- piece, so the sun was their only way to evaluate the time of day. After breakfast, the men had the three wagons ready. The first wagon was being pulled by two oxen; this was the one with the heavy load. The second wagon was pulled by two of the mules, and the third wagon had one ox. The convoy was ready.

Up front, Noah's wife held the bridle straps to the oxen. Noah was on horseback next to her wagon; he was the head scout. In the following wagon were Shem and his wife, and on the third wagon were Japheth and Ham's wives. On the back of the caravan were Ham and Japheth herding the domestic animals with the help of the dogs.

The voyage was slow as they moved down the hills. This took most of the day before they reached the flat land. Noah went on ahead to look for a place to rest themselves and the animals. He returned with good news; he gathered everyone to tell them that he had found a level area with a brook running through it. What a comfort this was to all; it was time to move on.

On the arrival of the caravan, everyone looked with amazement at the sight; there were hills to one side and a lake a distance away that was surrounded by a young forest of new trees. The birds that were following the caravan took to the forest.

The caravan came to rest, and everyone gathered to give thanks to the Lord God. Each family took a spot to lay their own tents. This took three hours. The men gathered wood from the roots left after the flood to build a fire. Japheth went to gather the herd, making sure they wouldn't wonder away and to feed the dogs that were guarding the animals. He was back in time to eat.

Noah and Ham build a rock altar to give thanks to God Jehovah for their journey. They all kneeled as Noah gave a burnt offering to God from what they had to eat. They had been there for some time and were comfortable, for this was to be their temporary home for some time to come. They had built a corral for the animals. Japheth was the caregiver of the animals.

One day, he was out in the field tending the flock. He had plenty of time trying to create things that would come in handy for them. He had a long leather strap wrapped around his waist when an idea snapped to his thoughts as what to do with the strap. He thought to himself, "I'll cut two lengths of the leather to the same length and place a piece of leather to the center where I can place a stone, so I can swing it around and around and be able to defend myself from hungry beasts."

When finished, he took it for a test. Around and around went the pouch with the rock in it. He struck it on a round cactus nearby and it smashed it beyond recognition. "Wow!" he exclaimed, "This will do fine."

He kept playing with it, when one of the straps slipped loose and the rock went flying quite a distance in front of him. He was amazed, so he stopped to think and again he tried it once more. Wow! His creative mind went to work.

He had quite a hard time getting used to releasing one strap and holding to the other, so he made a loop on one end for his finger, so the other end would release

freely. Time went by fast for him and realized it was time to return to camp.

When he arrived, he didn't say anything about what he had discovered; for him, it was just a moment of fun. His wife had warmed some water for him to refresh himself.

The family sat around, discussing the daily events and eating their supper. It was not determined how long they were to stay there, but Noah knew this was not the resting place God meant for them to make per- manent residence; and this was in his daily prayers.

Another day went by and everyone had something to do. Japheth, doing his job of tending the animals, was determined to improve his slinging. He found him- self able to get closer to his target, but it would take a while to maintain his accuracy.

Every day Japheth would practice; after a few weeks, he was able to hit his target at ninety-nine percent; now it was time to see if his sling would kill.

That morning, before he left, Noah told Japheth to bring a young mutton to cook for supper. He was warming up on his accuracy and he when up a way, Ham was coming up to visit with his little brother and to pick up the mutton. As he was approaching, he saw Japheth swinging what looked like a string with some- thing heavy on the end of the string. Japheth released the string at about twenty yards away. He hit the lamb behind the head, the lamb went down, and he shouted, "It works."

Unknown that his brother Ham was approaching him, Ham shouted out, "How did you do that?" Japheth proudly told his brother the story as to how

he came about the sling. Ham said, "Maybe you can show me how to use that thing?"

Japheth handed the sling to his brother, Ham started to swing the sling, around and around it went, when he released the loose end of the sling holding the stone, oops! The strap swung and wrapped around his leg. Ham screamed out, "*Ouch!* This is not for me."

They both started laughing and looking at Ham's leg. After cleaning and skinning the mutton and giving the remains to the dogs then burning the leftovers, the two started on their way back to the camp laughing hard over Ham's mishap.

At supper time, Ham just had to tell the story about what had happened to him, he said, "Father, with your permission, I have a story to tell all of you."

Noah saw the smiles on Ham and Japheth, and Noah replied, "I'm sure this is going to be good." He smiled as he looked at Ham and then over at Japheth. Ham continued, "As I was approaching Japheth, I noticed him swinging a string that had something in the pocket at the end. Suddenly, he released one end of the string that was holding a stone, and the stone slammed to the head of his target that we are eating right now. Yes! It is the mutton on the plate."

Everyone could not believe the story, just looking at each other. "I see doubt amongst all of you. Well, after supper I'm sure Japheth will put on a show with the skill he has received."

Noah had to say something. As he looked at Japheth and said, "Son, this seems to be cruel."

Japheth slowly replied, "Father, it seems crueler to slit the throat of the animal than a quick kill."

A silence came about. Noah thought it over and said, "You know son, you may have something there, but I don't know. This is not a toy and children may misuse it. We have to be careful not to expose this so-called 'sling' around them."

"Father, at your command it will be done."

The time had come for Japheth to demonstrate his skill. Ham placed three targets at quite a distance away. They also stood their distance as requested by Japheth. He picked up a stone, placed it in the pocket of the sling and commences to swing it. When releasing the sling, it popped as the stone flashed to the target. Next, was the second target, and then the third. What an exciting moment.

Shem had to say something to his little brother. "Japheth, the Lord has given you a good skill, but don't let it go to your head. You must be responsible with this weapon. The children are small now, but, what children see, they remember, so be careful."

Japheth replied. "I will obey."

The time had come for Grandpa Noah to tell the little ones a bedtime story, then on to bed. The last thing he said to them was a goodnight prayer. Later that night, Noah and Hancel were reminiscing and enjoying all that has happened since the day they left the ark. Noah asked her what she thought about Japheth's sling. It took her a moment to reply.

"Japheth has a level head on his shoulders, and he obeys you. I'm sure he will do right by what you told him."

Noah was satisfied.

Part 16

"You Must Move On."

Early one morning, Noah was praying at the stone altar when the voice of the Lord spoke to him. ***"Noah."***

Noah replied, "Here am I, my Lord."

"You and your family are outgrowing this area; you must move on, go beyond the lake that's before you, there, you will follow the river to the east, you will call the river Tigris, I'll be with you."

Noah stood, quietly thinking of how to go about this that the Lord has commanded him to do, and how he is to approach his family.

Noah's family had grown; he was now a grandfather to fifteen grandchildren and two more on the way. He decided to wait till suppertime when the whole family was together. That evening, after everyone had finished supper, it was time for Noah to speak. He said, "May I please have your attention?"

Everyone gave attention—even the children knew when grandfather spoke, it was time for them to listen.

He continued, "The Lord God spoke to me today. He told me that we must move on to beyond the great lake, and we are to follow the river he called The Tigris to the left, and on to the valley to the east."

Shem had to say something. "Father, we have set- tled here and are raising our children. We just can't move and leave all that we have sweated for, for so many years here."

Noah replied, "Son, this is not me who sent this request; it is the Lord's command, and we must obey. I have spoken."

No more was said.

Time was passing, and things were slow. Noah had to remind them once again. They gathered once more. Noah spoke again, "What must I have to tell you, can't you see? The stream is going dry. It is hard to even water the garden; look around you, the animals have grown in numbers and the land around us is losing its vege- tation. We must move on like God has ordered us to."

The boys gathered and discussed this over, for they knew they couldn't go against their father. Shem said, "Father, we will do as you say. What are we to do?"

"First thing we must do is to hang enough meat to sundry for us to carry with us; this the women can do. You all know we left many tools at the ark, so I was thinking, you, Shem, you and two of your older boys could go back to the ark and bring back the three saws and hammers and whatever you think we could use."

Shem said, "Papa, do you think the ark is safe?" Noah just looked at him. "I will get the boys ready and, in a day, or two we will be ready to travel."

It had been more than twenty years since they left the ark, and no one knew if the ark was still in one piece. The time was at hand. Shem and his two boys were ready to go back to the ark and retrieve what was needed. The rest of the family gathered many things and readied all that was to be taken with them. The wagon wheels were greased, and repairs were made. Two more wagons were added, with a two-wheel trailer in tow, now a total of seven. Shem took one of the large wagons with two horses, two dogs, and his two boys; they were on their way. The boys wanted to know what this thing called the ark was. Shem knew this trip was going to take a while, so he started to tell them the story. Many questions were asked by the boys. They had been on the road six hours.

By midday, they could see the ark from afar, but they still had a way to go. On arrival, Shem took note that the ark had slid a few feet. The ramp to the gate had also slid to the side, but it was still holding sturdy and he had no fear of any danger. He was able to take the wagon into the ark and then took the boys on a tour of the ark. It was so large that the boys were amazed. One of the boys asked, "Papa, you and grandpapa and uncle Ham and uncle Japheth built this thing? Wow! How long did it take to make it?"

He took the boys and sat them down and told them how the world had become so wicked and evil, and how God had told Papa Noah what was about to happen, and how it took many, many years to build. A short time later, he took the boys to the upper deck where the family had to stay during the flood.

There were many things that were still in good condi- tion and in good order after the length of time that had passed. It was time to eat and settle down for the night. It felt peaceful as they lay looking up at the stars from the only window the ark had. The dogs laid across the boys' legs. After the boys had gone to sleep, Shem went down to tend to the horses. He was surprised to see so much feed was still there and in good condition after that many years. He knelt and gave thanks to the Lord God and then he returned to where the boys were and fell asleep. The following morning, the sunlight was coming through the window above; they all woke up to a sunny day. Shem fed his boys and told them that they had to do some work and take anything they could see that was useful. The boys looked at this as a fun thing.

He said, "The first thing we must do is feed and water the animals. Then, we will look around and see where the tools are that we have to take with us." One of his boys located the tools in the second floor under the stairwell that went to the upper floor. Shem praised his sons. The wagon was filling up with many needed things.

It was time to check the upper section; there were many containers with grain and wheat; he saw two other unopened containers. He opened them, and to his surprise, salt! This was not supposed to have been left behind. Salt wasn't just for flavoring food, but it was also a good antiseptic. It took all day looking for what they needed. Now, it was time to eat. They had dry beef, sowbread, and dry fruit with a taste of salt. They had a wonderful time that turned out to be work, but Shem made it fun for the boys. Nightfall was approaching as they settled down for the night. Shem told his sons a story and they slowly fell asleep.

Morning came, and it was time to hitch the horses to the wagon to travel home. The load was somewhat heavy, and the road was downhill, so Shem had to be careful guiding the horses on foot. On the way down, they arrived at the creek they had passed when coming to the ark with no trouble, but the water had risen about two feet and it was hard to see the bottom. Sham had to stop the wagon and look things over. He had the boys help look for a different area where the water was passable. They looked downstream with no results. "Well, boys! It's time to go up stream." They laughed, turned, and started walking. They reached the wagon and walked on; they didn't go much more than what we call a block. Surprise, surprise: the stream was passable. They looked at each other and busted out laughing. The trip went well.

It was late afternoon when they arrived at the campsite. Everyone gathered around the wagon. Shem's wife was in tears with happiness to see her husband and her two boys back and safe. Noah was the most grateful, hoping Shem had found the missing tools needed. The wagon had more things than expected, not just the tools, but the salt that was more than welcomed. Shem also brought two bundles of cloth and blankets, three containers with wheat, and many seeds; all this was welcomed mostly by Hancel.

After the warm welcome, things were back to getting ready to travel in a day or two. One problem that was closely being watched was two of the women were with child. The women were Ham's wife and Japheth's wife. Ham's wife was close to her time and this worried Noah. A place was made for her; the women walked alongside the wagon, ready to help when the time came.

Next were the animals. The herd had multiplied from cows to goats and sheep, so did the chickens. Many of the children were old enough to help with the help of the fourteen dogs to guard the herd as they traveled on. There were thirty-four cows, forty sheep, and fif- ty-two goats. The chickens were placed on a wagon and pulled by two of the older boys. Everyone had a job to do. The lake that seemed to be so near turned out to be many days of travel. The time went by as they would sing along the way.

Part 17

A New Life Beyond the Lake

When the wagon-train arrived at the lakeside, it was time for everyone to take a bath. First, the little ones, which was easy since the kids love playing in the water. The elders separated; the man went one way the women went the other way.

The older kids took care of the little kids. After half a day of play and bathing, it was time to rest. Ham made a net and caught a few fish for dinner.

That night, everyone was having a great time when Ham's wife's time was at hand. A cry was heard, then another cry. Ham's wife had twins that evening. The caravan was delayed for two more months. The time at the lake was one of the happiest times for everyone. The animals were well rested and ready to travel once more. The wagon train was rolling once again.

The stories of the Bible tell about the different ter- rain that Noah's family had gone through; it has hot dry deserts, mountains, and green river valleys where many of the families had settled. The people of the deserts were nomads; they wondered around with their flocks. The people of the valley were farmers who settled down to cultivate the land. The caravan had traveled well over forty years stopping and moving on, looking for the Promised Land.

The families had grown quite large and many were ready to go on their own. Every time the caravan stopped, some of the growing family would stay and would become a small community. One settlement was called Nineveh and some years later, became a great city. One day the kids were paying in the mud, making mud squares and laid them to dry in the sun. When dried, they made little adobe huts noticed by Japheth who told the elders to come and see what the children were making with mud squares. After the showing the kids, this became a new way of making homes out of adobe brick.

Time was passing and the population growing rap- idly. A few years had passed and it was time for Noah and his sons move on. Some four hundred miles from their last stop at Nineveh, Noah and his sons followed their way along the Tigris River. They had many stops and much settlement along the way.

Following the Tigris River to the east is a large green valley with much vegetation which in time it was called Mesopotamia, a name which means, "the land between the two rivers" called, the Tigris and the Euphrates Rivers. This land had good fertile ground; and this was what Noah was looking for; he, being a farmer who lived from the land, found his paradise.

The Bible says in **Genesis 9:20** Noah planted a vineyard. It's unknown how long Noah resided in this area, other than one day he drank of the wine he had pressed and became intoxicated and lost control of his faculties, drunk!

I will leave it there; it's up to you to follow the story in the book of Genesis. All the days of Noah were 950 years; he died 359 years after the flood (Genesis 9:28).

This has been a wonderful word of origin and his- tory that the Lord has given me to share with you, when God placed this passage of **Luke 17:26-27** on my mind. **"But as the days of Noah were, so shell also be the coming of the Son of Man be."** When will all this come to pass? Only God knows; meanwhile, be thankful as you wait, and be careful what Bible you read, for evil has a way to confusing even the most **elect**. Remember: **people need the Lord.**

May the Lord God richly bless you.

These passages given to me by God: Those, God shall give to you by grace. So, shall the coming of the Lord.

"Take heed that no man deceives you;

For many shall come in my name saying, I am Christ: And shall deceive many."

So, says the Lord. **(Matthew 24:4) A-man.**

About the Author

My Name is Joseph N. Padilla.

I am a Christian book writer. I started writing my first book in 1957 I called "Adventure the Long Walk– After-Christ." It took me some forty years to finish; the reason it took me so long I lost confidence, it was my wife who convinced me to go on. She became ill and after many years I became her caregiver. She ended confined to her bed and a wheel-chair. In her last three years she was unable to speak, she communicated with me by writing notes. It was sad, but a beautiful unity between us for 53 years. One day she wrote me a note saying, "why don't you go back to your writing?" So, after forty years I took her advice. It took me a couple of years to finish the book. She passed on in

2005, she never got to see my novel. Writing stayed with me as I continued three more books including a children's novel called, Dragon Dee, and the Fire-man. Now My sixth book I call, "My Vision–A journey through Biblical Truth." This vision given to me I will interpret and make it simple to understand. It is the story of abomination that happened in the beginning onto the day Noah entered the ark that seem to be repeating today. I cannot tell why the Lord has placed this manu- script in my mind. The visions that come to me I cannot explain, so I sit and start writing: I have no papers or a degree in theology and I am a bad speller, yet my drive keeps on going. Everything that I write is found in the King James Bible. I comprehend the Word different than most. The interpretations that I write come to life as I go on.